Amazing Food Made Easy
Exploring Sous Vide

Consistently Create Amazing Food With Sous Vide

Jason Logsdon

Copyright © 2019 by Primolicious LLC

All rights reserved. Printed in the United States of America. No part of this book may be used or reproduced in any manner whatsoever without written permission except in the case of brief quotations embodied in critical articles and reviews.

For more information please contact Primolicious LLC at 12 Pimlico Road, Wolcott CT 06716.

ISBN-13: 978-1-945185-11-3

ISBN-10: 1-945185-11-2

Other Books By Jason Logsdon

Modernist Cooking Made Easy: Sous Vide

The Instant Pot Ultimate Sous Vide Cookbook

Simple Sous Vide

Amazing Food Made Easy: Healthy Sous Vide

Modernist Cooking Made Easy: Infusions

Modernist Cooking Made Easy: Getting Started

Modernist Cooking Made Easy: The Whipping Siphon

Modernist Cooking Made Easy: Party Foods

Sous Vide: Help for the Busy Cook

Sous Vide Grilling

Beginning Sous Vide

Table of Contents

Welcome to Exploring Sous Vide — 1

Sous Vide Overview — 3
The Sous Vide Process — 3
Recommended Sous Vide Equipment — 5
Ask Jason: Can You Reuse the Water? — 7

Key Safety Guidelines — 9
Stay Out of the Danger Zone — 9
Double Check the Circulator's Temperature — 10
Scientists Agree, Plastic Is Fine — 10
Always Pasteurize Certain Foods — 11

How Sous Vide Times Work — 13
Heat the Food — 13
Make the Food Safe to Eat — 14
Tenderize the Food — 16
Deep Look: Why the Range? — 18

Determining Temperature — 21
Effects of Sous Vide Temperature on Meat — 21
Determining Sous Vide Temperatures — 23

Before You Sous Vide — 27
Trimming, Shaping and Portioning Your Food — 27
Salting Before Sous Vide — 28
Seasoning Your Food Before Sous Vide — 29
Smoking Before Sous Vide — 30
Ask Jason: Should You Pre-Sear? — 31
Ask Jason: Should You Pre-Boil Meat? — 33

How to Seal Food — 35
What Does Sealing Actually Do? — 35
Types of Sous Vide Sealers — 36
Water Displacement Method — 38
How to Prevent Sous Vide Bags from Floating — 39
How Much Food Can I Put in a Bag? — 42
Ask Jason: Sous Vide in Store Packaging? — 43

How to Sear Food — 47
Prepping Food for Searing — 47
Ways of Searing Your Food — 48
Ask Jason: How to Keep Sous Vide Food Hot? — 50

Sous Viding in Bulk — 53
Benefits of Sous Viding in Bulk — 53
Bulk Sous Vide Process — 54
Freeze, Cook, Eat Method — 56
Cook, Freeze, Reheat Method — 56

Scheduling Sous Vide — 59
Stages of Sous Vide — 59
Day-Of Meats — 60
Multi-Day Meats — 62
Fast Cookers — 63
Cook, Chill, and Hold — 63
Deep Look: How to Delay a Sous Vide Cook — 64

Beef and Red Meat — 67
What Do I Mean by Red Meat? — 67
Pre-Sous Vide Preparation — 68
Sous Vide Temperatures for Red Meat — 69
Sous Vide Times for Red Meat — 71
How to Finish Red Meat — 72
Ask Jason: Steaks at Different Temperatures — 72
Hanger Steak with Succotash — 75
Chuck Steak w/ Asparagus and Shishito Peppers — 76
Short Rib Korean Lettuce Wraps — 78
Smoked Brisket with Bourbon BBQ Sauce — 80
Rack of Lamb w/ Pomegranate and Brussels Sprouts — 82
Bison Strip Steak Carbonara — 84

Pork and Boar — 87
Pre-Sous Vide Preparation — 87
Sous Vide Pork Temperatures — 88
Sous Vide Pork Times — 89
How to Finish Pork — 90
Pork Chops w/ Broccolini and Roasted Peppers — 91
Italian Sausage with Onions and Peppers — 92
Sous Vide St. Louis Ribs — 93
Pulled Pork with Chile Pepper BBQ Sauce — 94
Boar Tenderloin with Cherry Chutney — 96

Chicken, Duck and Poultry 99
What is Poultry? 99
Sous Vide Poultry Safety 100
Pre-Sous Vide Poultry Steps 100
How to Sous Vide Breast Meat 101
How to Sous Vide Dark Meat 103
How to Finish Poultry 103
Spring Salad with Chicken Breast 104
Honey-Sriracha Glazed Chicken Legs 106
Turkey Breast w/ Roasted Apples and Tomatoes 108
Duck Breast with Blackberry Port Sauce 110
Shredded Duck Legs with Sesame Noodles 112

Fish and Shellfish 115
Sous Vide Fish Safety 115
Pre-Sous Vide Fish Preparation 115
Sealing Sous Vide Fish 116
Sous Vide Fish Temperatures 116
Sous Vide Fish Times 117
How to Finish Fish 117
Ask Jason: What is "Sushi Quality" Fish 118
Shrimp and Quinoa Bowl 119
Swordfish in Dashi with Snow Peas 120
Sea Bass with Microgreens and Mustard Oil 122
Sesame Crusted Tuna with Avocado Salad 124
Lobster Tail with Tomato and Corn Salad 126

Vegetables and Fruits 129
Pre-Sous Vide Vegetable Preparation 129
Sealing Fruits and Vegetables 129
Vegetable Times and Temperatures 130
Asparagus with Dijon Mustard Vinaigrette 131
Miso Glazed Turnips 132
Curried Butternut Squash Soup 134
Chipotle Sweet Potato Salad 136
Apple Bourbon-Maple Chutney 137
Blueberry Compote 138

Infusions 141
Benefits of Sous Vide Infusions 141
How to Infuse with Sous Vide 141
How to Use Infused Alcohols 142
Strawberry Basil Infused Rum 143
Citrus Infused Oil 144
Cherry Vanilla Balsamic Vinegar 145

Eggs 147
What to Sous Vide Eggs In? 147
What Temperature to Sous Vide Eggs At? 148
13 Minute Egg on Wilted Spinach 149
Egg Cup Bites 150

Dairy, Grains and More 153
Cinnamon-Vanilla Crème Brulee 154
Sous Vide Yogurt 156

Equipment Links 159
Searing 159
Circulators 160
Containers, Clips and Racks 160
Sealers 161
Other 161

Cooking by Thickness 163
Cooking By Thickness 163
Thickness Times for Beef, Lamb and Pork 164
Thickness Times for Chicken and Poultry 166
Thickness Times for Fatty Fish 166

Cooking By Tenderness 169
Beef, Pork, Lamb and Other Meat 169
Chicken and Poultry 176
Fish and Shellfish 178
Fruit and Vegetable 179

Recipe Index 181

Did You Enjoy This Book? 182

About the Author 184

Endnotes 185

Welcome to Exploring Sous Vide

I'm so excited you've decided to take the next step and are committed to consistently creating amazing food using sous vide!

Sous vide isn't magic! Like most cooking methods, having the confidence to use it comes from a little bit of knowledge combined with practice.

Once you understand a surprisingly small amount of basic information, you will be able to trust yourself to regularly turn out amazing food with sous vide.

To help you get started, I've assembled all the information you need to know into this book. With sous vide you no longer have to cross your fingers and hope your food turns out perfect!

The book will start out with some introductions to the topics that I think every sous vider should know, which includes components of sous vide safety, how sous vide times and temperatures are determined, and an overview of the sous vide processes. They are designed to build your confidence in sous vide and help you trust the recipes you find on the internet. Hopefully both new and experienced sous vide cooks will learn a lot from them.

Then we'll dive into specific subjects in more depth such as searing techniques, detailed looks at different cuts of meat, options for sealing, and much more. I'll also share some of my favorite recipes and some helpful tools I've created to manage sous vide and sous vide times.

Throughout the book I'll intersperse short looks at specific questions I get asked a lot, such as when to salt, if you need to pre-boil your food, how quantity affects timing, and cooking foods to different temperatures in one bath.

I have also created a Facebook group called *Exploring Sous Vide*[1] to help us communicate, so if you have questions or comments, you can post to that group so everyone can benefit. And please don't hesitate to reach out to me with questions, concerns, or comments at jason@afmeasy.com.

I look forward to exploring sous vide with you!

Sous Vide Overview

I want to start by going over the sous vide process and the equipment needed for sous vide. It can be helpful to have an overview whether you are new to sous vide or just want a recap of how it works.

In future chapters we will dive into each aspect of sous vide and the equipment used in more detail, but I want to first provide an overview so you know what to expect.

The Sous Vide Process

There are a few variations on the process, but in general you determine the time and temperature you want to cook your food for. Next you season and seal your food in sous vide bags. Then you place the bags in a water bath that is held to the specific temperature and let it cook. Finally, you remove it from the water bath and the pouch, then finish it off, usually by searing.

Determine the Time and Temperature

There are many factors that go in to determining the time and temperature you will use to cook sous vide but in general, the temperature determines how "done" the meat is and the time affects how tender it becomes. This combination of time and temperature is used with different cuts of meat in several ways.

Heat Tender Foods

For tender foods, you just need to cook them long enough to heat them through, and sometimes pasteurize them. So filet mignon, pork chops, and chicken breasts only need to be cooked for a few hours at the temperature you want to eat them at.

This is usually 130°F to 140°F (54.5°C to 60°C) for beef, 135°F to 145°F (57.5°C to 62.5°C) for pork and 140°F to 150°F (60°C to 65.5°C) for white poultry meat.

Tenderize Tough Foods

For foods that are tougher, such as a chuck roast, pork shoulder, or short ribs, you need to cook the meat long enough for it to tenderize and break down. This is the same concept as with traditional cooking, there is a reason you traditionally smoke or braise these cuts and don't just toss them on the grill. You need long cooking times at lower temperatures to break down the meat.

The amount of time it takes to break the meat down is dependent on the temperature you are cooking it at. A chuck roast cooked at 131°F (55°C) will take 36 to 48 hours to fully tenderize, while at 185°F (85°C) it happens in 12 hours.

However, the 131°F chuck roast will have the texture and flavor of a good steak while the 185°F chuck roast will be fall-apart tender like a braise. So the temperature you pick will make a huge difference in the flavor and texture of the final dish.

Pre-Sous Vide Preparation and Sealing

Once you've determined the time and temperature you want to use, the next step in the sous vide process is to get the food ready to cook. This generally includes adding spice rubs and sealing the food in a sous vide pouch but it can also encompass brining, smoking, marinating, and other methods of adding flavor to food.

Once the food is seasoned you seal it in a sous vide pouch, typically a Ziploc freezer bag (my favorite method) or in a FoodSaver or vacuum sealer pouch. The sealing is important to ensure the food heats evenly and that the water is as close to the meat as possible.

Heat Up Some Water and Cook the Food

Once the food is sealed, you set your sous vide machine to the temperature you picked. Once the water is heated, place the sealed sous vide pouch in the water and let it cook.

There are many ways to keep the temperature consistent, from using a thermometer on the stove up to buying an immersion circulator. Circulators have dropped in price significantly over the years and I now recommend the Sansaire, Anova or Gourmia because they are inexpensive and work well. I also recommend the Joule for more tech-heavy fans of sous vide.

Finish with a Sear

Once the food has been cooked for as long as you want, you remove the pouch from the water bath and finish the food. This usually entails removing it from the pouch, drying it off, and then searing it to add a flavorful crust. The searing can be done in a hot pan, on a grill, or even with a sous vide torch like I prefer. Once the food is seared it's all ready to plate and eat!

That's really all there is to the sous vide process, everything else is just nuance and personal preference. Over the rest of this book I'll help you understand how time and temperature work to cook your food perfectly every time so you can consistently create amazing food with sous vide. I'll also provide many simple recipes for everyday food that looks and tastes great.

Recommended Sous Vide Equipment

I get a lot of questions about what type of equipment is needed for sous vide. While you can do short sous vide cooks using nothing but a pot, a thermometer and a stove, there are several pieces of equipment that make sous vide much easier.

There are three areas of sous vide equipment, they include ones for sealing the food, heating the water, and searing the food. I'll give you my recommendations for each here and provide links to all this equipment and more in the Equipment Links chapter.

> **Note:** Sous vide equipment is constantly changing and evolving. I highly recommend checking out my online[2] equipment reviews to see what my latest recommendations are.

Sealing Sous Vide Food

Even though "sous vide" means "under vacuum", the only important part of sealing your food is to remove as much air as possible. This allows the water to come in closer contact with the food which transfers the heat more efficiently. There are several ways you can accomplish this.

Ziploc Freezer Bags and Sous Vide

The first and easiest way to seal your food is to simply use Ziploc brand freezer bags. This is what I use for a lot of my cooks because they are really easy to use and there's not a machine taking up valuable counter space. You can use the water displacement method discussed in the How to Seal Food chapter to get the air out and you are good to go. I also have a video on my website of the process[3].

Using the "freezer" bags ensures that the bags hold up well to the higher temperatures used in sous vide.

Vacuum Sealers

For a tighter seal on your food, many people turn to vacuum sealers. These come as either edge-sealers like the FoodSaver and Oliso brands, or a chambered vacuum sealer like the VacMaster. These can be great to use if you already own one or if you do a lot of food storage, though you don't need them to get started.

I prefer vacuum bags like these for cooks over 12 hours or at higher temperatures. The bags seem to hold up a little bit better and have less of a chance of leaking.

Heating Water with Sous Vide

The most critical piece of sous vide equipment is the device that heats your water. There's a lot of different types of machines but I generally recommend a sous vide circulator. They are relatively inexpensive now (under $200) and there are several options, with more coming out every day. For the most up-to-date machines, please check out the sous vide machine review[4] or the sous vide benchmarks[5] pages on my website.

After testing most of the ones available I now use the Sansaire because it is a little quieter than the others (important in a small NY apartment) and heats slightly faster (important when it takes 15 minutes for your faucet to heat up). Both my dad and my mother-in-law have settled on the Anova. Many people also use the Gourmia Sous Vide Pod, which comes with a booklet of my recipes, and the Joule is a new-comer to the scene and very popular.

We all use them with a Cambro 12 quart container to hold the water. We also have cut a hole in the lid to prevent evaporation. Lipavi also makes several great sous vide containers with pre-cut lids.

Searing After Sous Vide

There are many ways to sear your food after you have finished cooking it with sous vide. If you are getting started, go ahead and just pan fry your food. It's the cheapest method since you probably already have a pan and a stove. Many people rave about using cast iron pans as well.

I often use a BernzOmatic torch to sear my food. It works more quickly than the stove, results in less over cooking, and has less clean up. Many people use the Searzall attachment as well.

We will go in to much more depth about these various tools in the How to Sear Food chapter.

Ask Jason: Can You Reuse the Water?

"I feel like there is so much water wasted with sous vide cooking, do I really need to change it every time I cook? How clean is the water once I'm done, can I do anything with it?"–Joshua H

A lot of us are in the situation where we don't have to think too much about the water we are using. However, many people aren't that lucky or have made the conscious decision to be more conservationally minded in their thinking.

For people trying to reduce their water use there are several options you can implement. This includes using a smaller amount of water initially, using the water for multiple cooks, and re-using the water for other purposes once you are done cooking with it.

Use Less Water During Sous Vide

The first step to reducing water usage is to just use enough water to cover your food and not always fill up the container every time. This is easier on shorter cooks when you don't have evaporation concerns, but similar principals can be applied on longer cooks if you cover your water bath.

You can also use containers of different sizes to minimize water usage. There are many sous vide containers that come in all sizes. If you are just cooking for one or two people you can probably get away with a much smaller size than if you are cooking for a group of friends.

Just make sure there is enough room for the water to circulate and maintain the temperature evenly throughout the water bath. I generally try not to have the food take up more than half the volume of the container.

Use the Water for Multiple Cooks

If you sous vide more than once or twice a week you don't have to empty your water bath container in between each one. Even if the water isn't completely clean it's not a big deal because the food is always sealed in a sous vide bag.

How long you feel comfortable going between cooks is up to you, but I generally just replace my water every 10 to 15 days. Of course, if a bag leaks you need to take that in to account.

Many people suggest adding something to help kill anything that might grow in the water. This can be a few drops of bleach, some vinegar, or something like "pool shock" which is rated as safe for humans and designed specifically to kill things that grow in room temperature water.

Use the Water for Other Things

Just because you are emptying your water bath doesn't mean you have to pour it down the drain. If the water is fresh and your sous vide bags didn't have a leak many people use it to wash or soak their dishes at the end of the meal.

It's also very common for people to let the water cool and then use it to water their plants.

Some people even cool off the water and then use it to water their dogs or drink it themselves, though that's a little too hard core for me!

Key Safety Guidelines

If there's one thing you need to know when cooking, whether it is using sous vide or any other technique, it is what procedures are important for you to follow to be safe when preparing your food.

I've put together a list of the top safety points in regards to sous vide. If you follow them, you won't get sick according to the US Government, Harold McGee, Douglas Baldwin, and Serious Eats, whose more scientific-based leads I follow.

Before I start though, I think it's important to point out that sous vide is no more or less safe than other methods of cooking. There's a lot of talk about the safety of sous vide, but it's just as easy to make yourself sick by under-cooking a chicken in the oven or not pasteurizing grilled pork. So don't be intimidated, once you know a few rules of thumb you will be all set.

Stay Out of the Danger Zone

From a safety standpoint, food cooking at temperatures below 130°F (54.4°C) isn't being cooked at all, it's just being warmed up. The bacteria we are trying to remove from cooking thrive from around 40°F to 126°F (4.4°C to 52.2°C), and they stop growing but don't start dying quickly until around 130°F (54.4°C). That range is known as the "danger zone" (cue Top Gun music) and it's often referred to in food safety circles.

> **Note:** Sometimes the danger zone is even considered to be up to 140°F (60°C) but that is based on building in a margin of error for restaurants, not the actual growth and death of the pathogens.

Cooking a piece of meat below 130°F (54.4°C) is the equivalent to letting it sit on your counter. It's fine for a few hours but it's not something you'll want to do all day. A generally accepted safe overall time in the danger zone, from leaving the fridge through cooking and eating is generally considered 3 to 4 hours.

Any piece of food that needs cooked longer than a few hours should be cooked at a minimum temperature of 130°F (54.4°C). If there is only one thing to remember about cooking in general, and sous vide cooking specifically, it's to not have your food between 40°F (4.4°C) and 130°F (54.4°C) for more than a few hours.

For a really good look at this process, as well as many other scientific underpinnings of cooking, I highly recommend On Food and Cooking by Harold McGee.

Double Check the Circulator's Temperature

Most sous vide circulators are very precise and the temperature does not fluctuate much at all. However, they can sometimes become uncalibrated and then heat to the wrong temperature, usually only by a degree or two.

If you push the limits of the danger zone, that degree could be the difference between safe food and unsafe food.

Because of this potential calibration issue, it's good to double check the temperature of your circulator every few weeks with another thermometer. I also recommend cooking a degree or two above the danger zone for all cooks over a few hours unless you have just calibrated your machine. If you must push the danger zone, I highly suggest getting a second thermometer that you can use to double check the temperature of the water.

Scientists Agree, Plastic Is Fine

A main concern of sous vide safety is cooking in plastic and whether or not this is a dangerous practice. Many scientists and chefs believe that cooking in food-safe, BPA-free plastic at these low temperatures does not pose any risk, the temperature is about equivalent to leaving a bottle of water in your car, or in a semi-truck during transport in summer. This included Ziploc freezer bags, sous vide bags, and most food-safe plastics.

However, I find it hard to believe that we know everything about how plastic reacts to heat, water, our bodies, and the environment. As such, I encourage you to read up on the safety of plastic in sous vide and plastic in general and come to your own conclusions about the safety of using these techniques.

I hope this will at least give you some various perspectives on it and you can make an informed opinion of your own.

Note: For some more information, I recommend reading posts by Modernist Cuisine[6] and Chef Steps[7].

Always Pasteurize Certain Foods

Sometimes when cooking you want to ensure your food is pasteurized, not just heated through. This is particularly important for chicken and poultry, blade-tenderized steaks, and low quality fish.

Pasteurization occurs when the food is held at a specific temperature for a certain amount of time. The higher the temperature is, the faster the food is pasteurized. Even though the temperatures in the chart below range from barely medium-rare to medium-well they are all equally safe to eat when cooked for the indicated times.

These times all start once the middle of the piece of meat has reached the indicated temperature. I will talk more about it in the next chapter, but you can use the charts in the Cooking by Thickness chapter to determine how long it takes to reach the indicated temperature.

The "recommended cooking times" that the US Government puts out are designed to produce pasteurized food instantly. For example, at the generally recommended chicken temperature of 165°F (73.8°C) it will be pasteurized in less than a second. That short amount of time is why the government recommends it, so if a cook pulls a piece of chicken off the grill right as it hits the temperature, it'll still be safe to eat. But chicken cooked to 165°F (73.8°C) and held for one second, is just as safe as chicken cooked to 140°F (60.0°C) and held for 30 minutes.

Once Heated, Beef is Pasteurized at
- 130°F (54.4°C) for 2 hours
- 133°F (56.1°C) for 1 hour
- 138°F (58.9°C) for 18 minutes
- 145°F (62.8°C) for 4 minutes

Once Heated, Chicken is Pasteurized at
- 140°F (60.0°C) for 30 minutes
- 145°F (62.8°C) for 12 minutes
- 150°F (65.6°C) for 4 minutes

Warning: It is very important to always pasteurized food when you are serving it to immuno-compromised people. This generally includes pregnant women, the elderly, babies, or those with weak immune systems.

How Sous Vide Times Work

When determining how long to sous vide certain items the confusion often comes down to the difference between cooking by thickness and cooking by tenderness. I want to take a more in-depth look at those types of cooking to help clear up any uncertainty around them.

When cooking food, either via sous vide or traditional methods, there are three goals: heat the food; make the food safe to eat; and tenderize the food.

I'll take a look at each one of the goals, discuss how it relates to the other goals, and tie it in to how sous vide times and temperatures are determined. At the end, you should understand why different cuts of meat have different time requirements, even if they are the same size.

In the discussion below, we will use a 1" thick chicken breast (25mm), a 1" beef filet (25mm), and a 1" chuck steak (25mm) to highlight the differences.

Heat the Food

When it comes right down to it, the whole purpose of cooking is to heat the food. Heating the food has several benefits including increasing the flavor, making the food safe, and breaking down the tough fibers in the food.

Regardless of the reason, adding heat to food is arguably the most critical component of cooking.

With traditional cooking, your food has a temperature gradient to it, popularly referred to as the "bulls-eye effect". This is because cooking at high temperatures overcooks the outside of the food while the inside of the food is heating up. Because of this discrepancy, it is hard to accurately judge when a piece of food will be fully heated through with a traditional cooking method.

With the precision and static temperatures used in sous vide cooking, you can predict how long it will take the center of a piece of food to come up to temperature to within a good degree of accuracy. There are a few variables including the density of the meat and water temperature, but most meat heats through roughly at the same pace regardless of the water bath temperature or the minor density differences between steak and chicken. Fatty fish is one of the few foods that heats pretty differently.

To help you out, you can view the tables in the Cooking by Thickness chapter to determine the amount of time it takes to heat up a piece of meat. It has a detailed listing for different thicknesses of red meat as well as chicken, and fish. You can also download my sous vide thickness ruler[8] that you can print out and use at home.

Because all meat heats in about the same time frame, all three of our example pieces of meat would heat up in about an hour and 15 minutes, regardless of the temperature.

However, if we had cooked them all at 131°F (55°C) then, despite being the same temperature, they would taste very different. The beef filet would be perfectly cooked and tasty after a quick sear because it is already a tender piece of meat. The chuck steak would be very chewy, because it is a tough cut and wasn't tenderized at all. And the chicken would not be safe to eat, since it would not have become pasteurized yet.

Make the Food Safe to Eat

While the information I discuss in this section normally only comes up in discussions about sous vide, they actually apply to all forms of cooking. Many people do not understand them (though they think they do) and this can lead to generally unsafe cooking practices, overcooked food, and other issues. Just one more benefit of being familiar with sous vide...you'll be more informed and safe in your general cooking as well.

As I mentioned in the previous chapter, the main concern with making food safe to eat is "pasteurization". Pasteurized food has had the amount of dangerous bacteria and parasites in it reduced to acceptable levels (the US Government suggests killing all but 1 in a million, or 1 in 10 million, depending on the pathogen).

Pasteurized food is then generally safe to eat, provided it is eaten within a few hours so the remaining bacteria do not have time to re-grow. Pasteurization is achieved by holding food at a specific temperature for a certain length of time, with higher temperatures resulting in faster pasteurization.

When to Pasteurize Meat

Some meat needs to be fully pasteurized, and other types of meat are safe to eat as long as you sear them.

There are a variety of factors that go in to whether or not you need to pasteurize a type of meat, including the conditions the animals were raised (factory farmed meat and wild game both introduce different risks) but I'll focus on standard types of meat generally found in US supermarkets. If you are eating an unusual type of meat, or wild game, then it is best to pasteurize it just to be safe.

Pork is often pasteurized as well, though high quality pork is usually fine without being pasteurized.

When deciding whether or not to pasteurize your food, you need to worry about parasites and bacteria. Different types of meat have different parasites, and the bacteria also behaves differently depending on the density of the food.

When to Pasteurize Chicken and Poultry with Sous Vide

Chicken and other poultry should always be pasteurized since the bacteria can penetrate to the inside of the meat. Because of this penetration, the entire piece of meat needs to be heated through and pasteurized. This is why chicken tartar or medium-rare chicken is never served. Through sous vide, you can actually pasteurize chicken at a medium-rare temperature, but I'm not a fan of the texture.

When to Pasteurize Beef and Lamb with Sous Vide

Denser meats like beef, lamb, and duck breast are too dense for the bacteria to penetrate below the surface. This means that to make them safe to eat, all you need to do is heat the surface, usually through searing it.

That heat applied to the outside effectively pasteurizes it because the inside is considered sterile. You can also remove the surface, which is often done when there is no cooking involved, such as with tartar.

Therefore, as long as you sear the outside, the inside can stay whatever temperature you prefer. A well-done steak is no safer to eat than a just-briefly-seared rare steak, neither will have any bacteria inside. This is why with our example cuts the beef heated through was safe to eat but the chicken wasn't.

It's important to remember this only stays true when the outside of the meat is really the outside. For example, if you grind the meat for hamburgers, the outside is now on the inside and a sear won't fix that.

> **Note:** I particularly liked this video that describes why beef is safe to eat when eaten at lower temperatures: https://youtu.be/hfSVH8f-C3I

This is the reason hamburgers are rarely served medium-rare, cooking the outside doesn't make the inside safe. Special precautions must be taken when serving under-cooked ground beef, such as using only high quality beef, and sterilizing or trimming off the outside before grinding.

Another time when the outside can become the inside is with "blade tenderized" or "jaccard" steaks. These steaks are tenderized by pushing blades though them, which also carry bacteria to the inside. Many Costco steaks utilized this method, and it leads to potential sickness if those steaks aren't pasteurized during cooking.

> **Warning:** It is also worth mentioning again that for immuno-compromised individuals like the elderly and pregnant women it is best to pasteurize all food.

How to Pasteurize with Sous Vide

The amount of time something needs to be cooked is dependent on both the type of meat and the heat it is cooked at. For our 1" (25mm) beef and chicken examples, they will be pasteurized if they were cooked as follows.

> **1" Beef Steak Pasteurized at**
> 131°F (55°C) for 2 hours and 45 minutes
> 135°F (57°C) for 1 hour and 50 minutes
> 140°F (60°C) for 1 hour and 20 minutes
>
> **1" Chicken Breast Pasteurized at**
> 136°F (58°C) for 2 hours and 20 minutes
> 140°F (60°C) for 1 hour and 40 minutes
> 149°F (65°C) for 1 hour

For time and temperature combinations, you can refer to the Cooking by Thickness chapter then go to the type of food you are interested in. Also, if you are a sucker for partial differential equations, then Douglas Baldwin[9] provides a lot more information on pasteurization and the specific pathogens you are trying to kill, including his mathematical models behind it.

If we cooked our example cuts for the amount of time listed above they would all be perfectly safe to eat, even if they had been blade tenderized. Both the beef filet and chicken breast would be ready to eat and would taste delicious. However, the chuck steak would still be really chewy and tough, which leads us to our third reason to heat food: tenderization.

Tenderize the Food

The third reason to heat food is to tenderize it. As food gets hot, the muscle, collagen, and protein undergo transformations that cause the food to get more and more tender. The higher the temperature the food is cooked at, the faster this tenderization happens. This is why pressure cooked foods cook faster than roasted or braised food.

Like braising or roasting, the longer you cook food with sous vide the more tender it becomes. The main difference is that adding time to sous vide cooking doesn't overcook the outside layers of the food.

Also, because the sous vide temperatures are so low, the tenderization happens much more slowly, resulting in much longer cooking times. To really enjoy that chuck steak, you'll want to cook it for about two days.

The upside of using the lower temperatures is that you can cook your food to any doneness you want. If you braise a roast, it will always turn out well-done, but using sous vide allows you to turn out a perfectly medium-rare roast that is still tender.

This is possible because using the temperature control of sous vide allows you to break down and tenderize meat without cooking it above medium-rare and drying it out. Once temperatures in beef go above 140°F (60°C) the meat begins to dry out and become blander. Using sous vide, you can hold the meat below 140°F (60°C) for a long enough time for the tenderizing process to run its course.

The length of time needed for cooking increases as the food gets tougher and the temperature you are cooking it at gets lower. Here are some general guidelines which will vary a little by the specific cut.

Common Sous Vide Times
Tender Beef: 1 to 4 hours
Tough Beef: 10 to 24+ hours
Tender Pork: 2 to 8 hours
Tough Pork: 12 to 48 hours
White Chicken: 2 to 4 hours
Dark Chicken: 4 to 8 hours

After 36 to 48 hours our example chuck steak would be fully tenderized and have a texture similar to a filet or ribeye. The tenderization continues to happen throughout the cooking process though, so if our tender beef filet was cooked for the same 48 hours as the chuck steak, it would have little internal structure and taste very mushy.

Compared to traditional methods there is actually a lot of wiggle room though, so the filet would still be good for a few hours after it was heated.

You can view my comprehensive sous vide times and temperatures in the Cooking by Tenderness chapter at the back of the book for more specific recommendations. In the next chapter I will take a much longer look at how temperature affects food and how it is combined with times to create good meals.

DEEP LOOK: Why the Range?

One of the most common questions I get asked about my sous vide recipes is some variation of "the recipe says to cook it for 3 to 6 hours, but when is it actually done".

The short answer is that anytime within the given range the food is "done".

As long as the food has been in the water bath for more than the minimum time and less than the maximum time, then it is done. There isn't a specific magical moment of true doneness that can be generalized.

For those that want more information, here's the explanation why.

The How and Why of Sous Vide Time Ranges

To have this conversation we first need to determine what "done" actually means. For sous vide there are two main "doneness" concerns when cooking your food. The first is to ensure that the food actually comes up to the temperature you are cooking it at. Or for some foods like chicken and poultry, to ensure it stays at that temperature long enough for it to become pasteurized and safe to eat.

The second concern is making sure the food is tender enough to eat without being "over tender", mushy, or dry.

Once the food you are cooking is completely up to temperature for a long enough time to be safe to eat, and it has tenderized enough to eat, it is now "done".

For some already tender cuts of meat like filets, loins, and chicken breasts you don't have to worry about tenderness since they start out that way. This means these cuts are "done" once they get up to temperature and/or are pasteurized. You can find out this time using the charts in the Cooking by Thickness chapter.

However, despite them being "done" at the minimum time shown, they stay "done" for several hours past that time, depending on the starting tenderness of the meat. This is why I give a range. You can eat a 1" cut of filet mignon (25mm) after 50 minutes but you can also eat the filet up to 3 hours after it has been placed in the bath without any loss in quality, tenderness, or flavor.

This is how my ranges are determined. They specify that for an average cut of the given meat, they will become "great to eat" tender at the minimum time given. They will continue to get more tender the longer they are in the bath but will remain "great to eat" tender until the final time given, at which point they may begin to get mushy and overcooked. In essence, they will be "done", and very tasty, for that entire span between the minimum and maximum times.

Another Way to Look at It

Another way to think about how this works is to use the following analogy. Pretend you were helping a new cook grill a steak. If they told you they wanted to cook it medium rare and asked you how to tell when it was "done", what would you say? Most people would reply with "When the temperature is between 131°F to 139°F" (55°C to 59.4°C).

If the friend isn't a cook they would ask "Yeah, but when is it actually done?"

The answer at this point really comes down to personal preference since to some people medium-rare is perfect at 131°F (55°C) and others prefer it a little more well-done at 135°F (57°C), but a medium-rare steak is "done" anywhere in that range.

Other Critical Variables

One other complicating factor is the many variables that go in to determining how fast a piece of meat tenderizes and/or becomes tender.

The most obvious variable is that some cuts of meat are tougher than others. For example, a top round roast needs to be tenderized a lot longer than a ribeye. Most people realize this so almost all sous vide charts break the food down by "cut".

Another less obvious but almost as important factor is where the meat came from. There is a big difference between how fast the meat tenderizes and how the cow was raised. I've found that grass-fed meat from my local farmer needs just half the time to become tender compared to supermarket meat (this is also true when roasting or braising them). I've also talked to a reader in Mexico who eats local grass-fed beef that needs slightly longer times than normal because the cows work more.

There are also the variables in the actual cow itself. Whether the meat is prime, choice, or select makes a difference in tenderizing time. As does the marbling, how old the meat is, and several other factors.

When you take all of this together it can be hard to accurately determine a range of "doneness" that will work for all cuts of meat. But I try my best to come up with a nice range of times that the "average" piece of meat will be done in. The only way to really learn is to experiment with the types of meat in your area and see how they react.

And luckily for us, sous vide allows us to have a wide range that food is done in.

In Conclusion

So while there might be one magical moment in the cooking process where a certain piece of meat is the most ideal tenderness, in practice there is a wide time range in the cooking process where the meat will be "done". As long as you take it out some time in that range it should turn out great.

As you get more experience with your local meats, and determine your personal preferences, you can start to tweak your cook times to suit them more exactly. But as you are learning, just remember that the food will be "done" anywhere in that range, and don't sweat the details!

Determining Temperature

The most important thing to know when trying to consistently create amazing food with sous vide is understanding how time and temperature work together to cook your food. In the previous chapter, we talked about how sous vide times work and now we will look at sous vide temperatures.

As opposed to most traditional cooking methods, sous vided food is cooked at the temperature you want the final food to end up at. This is usually between 120°F and 185°F (48.9°C and 85°C), depending on the food being prepared.

There are a few different categories of food, but in this chapter I will focus on meat. It applies to beef, lamb and pork, as well as poultry and game meats. Later chapters will cover vegetables, infusions, custards, and other foods.

Effects of Sous Vide Temperature on Meat

Viewed from a high-level perspective, as meat is heated the components that make it up change. These changes result in structural transformations that affect the texture, juiciness, and mouth-feel of the meat. The higher the temperature of the heat applied to the meat, the faster these changes occur.

As proteins are heated, they begin to contract. This contraction squeezes moisture out of the meat, which is one reason well-done steaks are so dry.

On the flip side, when collagen is heated, it breaks down, releasing gelatin and resulting in tender meat, which is one reason pot roasts and braises are fall-apart tender. Choosing the right temperature for what you are trying to accomplish is critical to consistently creating amazing food.

Note: The following examples are mainly of beef, but the concepts also hold true for most red meats, pork, and poultry.

As meat is heated above 120°F (48.9°C) it starts to tenderize. The meat also starts to become firmer, but with minimal moisture loss.

Above 140°F (60°C) the meat quickly starts to lose moisture as it contracts, resulting in much firmer meat.

Above 160°F (71.1°C) almost all moisture is removed from the meat as it clumps together. However, collagen also begins breaking down quickly, adding a lubricating gelatin and creating a "fall-apart" texture.

This breakdown of collagen is why many traditionally cooked tough cuts of meat are braised or roasted for a long period of time, insuring the meat can fully tenderize.

However, because of the high temperatures they can easily become dried out. Using sous vide allows you to hold the meat below the 140°F (60°C) barrier long enough for the slower tenderization process to be effective. This results in very tender meat that is still moist and not overcooked.

For the curious, I wrote a more detailed look at How Does Temperature Affect Meat[10].

As discussed in the chapter on Key Safety Guidelines, it is unsafe to cook below 130°F (54.4°C) for more than about four hours. This is why most tough cuts of meat are cooked at or above 130°F (54.4°C). In order to cook them long enough for the tenderization to work, you need to cook them for a much longer time than 4 hours...some of the toughest cuts are cooked for up to 3 days.

Determining Sous Vide Temperatures

More than any other factor, the temperature used in sous vide determines the end result of the food. Different temperatures will produce food with extremely different textures, and understand which temperatures do what is key.

It's common to focus on the precision of sous vide machines and get bogged down discussing exact temperatures.

Many people argue if a steak should be cooked at 130°F or 131°F (54.4°C or 55°C) and to me it is just overkill. There is a difference between degrees, but especially when just getting started I find it best to think in terms of ranges of temperature since each range results in very similar food.

An example is comparing a medium-rare steak to a braised pot roast. The steak is moist, bright red, with a little chew to it. The pot roast is brown, dry (except for the wonderful juices in the braise liquid), and is pull-apart tender.

We've all had steaks cooked to different temperatures, even ones that we would still consider "medium-rare", and they are all basically the same type of dish, especially when compared to the pot roast.

The medium-rare range goes from around 130°F to 139°F (54.4°C to 59.4°C) for beef. As long as you set your sous vide machine in that range, you'll get a great medium-rare meal. Once you've tried it a few times you can decide if you prefer 131°F or 132°F, but that's not critical to getting started successfully.

This personal preference is where a lot of differences in recommended recipe temperatures come from. Some people prefer their steaks a little more done at 135°F (57.2°C) and some people love them at 130°F (54.4°C), but one temperature isn't "right" for everyone.

Common Sous Vide Temperatures

Picking a temperature is as easy as figuring out what kind of meat you want and selecting any number in that range. Once you have tried out a few different temperatures you can get a feel for what you prefer.

Here are some of the more common ranges I use when determining what temperature to cook food at.

Medium-Rare Beef
130°F-139°F (54.4°C-59.4°C)

Medium Beef
140°F-145°F (60°C-62.8°C)

Traditional "Slow Cooked" Beef
156°F-175°F (68.8°C-79.4°C)

Extra-Juicy Tender Pork
135°F-145°F (57.2°C-62.8°C)

Traditional Tender Pork
145°F-155°F (62.8°C-68.3°C)

Traditional "Slow Cooked" Pork
156°F-175°F (68.8°C-79.4°C)

Extra-rare Chicken Breast
136°F-139°F (57.7°C-59.4°C)

Traditional Chicken Breast
140°F-150°F (60°C-65.6°C)

Mi-cuit Fish
104°F (40°C)

Traditional Fish
122°F-132°F (50°C-55.5°C)

Common Times and Temperatures

Once you've picked a temperature you like, you can then combine it with the sous vide times we learned about in the last chapter.

These are simplified but should get you started on your way. You can look for specific examples in my online sous vide recipes[11] or read the Cooking by Thickness and Cooking by Tenderness chapters at the back of the book for more specific recommendations.

Tender Beef and Lamb 1.5" Thick or Less
Medium-Rare: 131°F (55°C) for 2 hours
Medium: 140°F (60°C) for 2 hours

Tough Beef and Lamb Roasts
Medium-Rare: 131°F (55°C) for 48 hours
Medium: 140°F (60°C) for 48 hours
Traditional "slow cooked" beef: 161°F (71.7°C) for 36 hours

Tender Pork 1.5" Thick or Less
Extra-Juicy Pork: 140°F (60°C) for 3 hours
Traditional Pork: 145°F (62°C) for 3 hours

Tough Pork
"Chop Like" Pork: 145°F (62°C) for 24 hours
Traditional "Slow Cooked" Pork: 165°F (73.9°C) for 24 hours

Pork Ribs
Tender Ribs: 141°F (60.6°C) for 24 hours
Traditional "Slow Cooked" Ribs: 156°F (68.8°C) for 12 hours

Chicken, Turkey, and Poultry
White Meat: 141°F (60.6°C) for 3 hours
Dark Meat: 148°F (64.4°C) for 3 hours
Duck Breast: 130°F (54.4°C) for 2 hours

Fish
Mi-cuit: 104°F (40°C) for 40 minutes
Cooked: 122°F (50°C) for 40 minutes
Flaky: 132°F (55.5°C) for 40 minutes

Before You Sous Vide

In the world of sous vide, there's a whole lot of talk about what circulator to buy, how to seal your food, and what's the best way to get a good sear. Those are all very important parts of the process but many people forget about the pre-sous vide preparation, the stuff that happens before you bag your food.

The main task you are trying to accomplish during the pre-sous vide preparation is to make your food taste better. This generally involves the addition of spices and herbs, but it can also take the form of transformational methods such as brining, portioning, or even pre-boiling. We will look at many of these processes in more depth.

Trimming, Shaping and Portioning Your Food

Many types of food can benefit from some prep work before you cook them. This can include some initial trimming, shaping and portioning.

Trimming Food Before Sous Vide

Many cuts of meat cook much better with some initial trimming, such as removing the membrane from ribs or the silver skin from pork tenderloin. This is best to do before you season or bag them since the food is easier to work with (and you're not holding up dinner!).

Also, since sous vide does not get up to high temperatures for most meats, it does not render fat nearly as well as other cooking techniques. Unless you are cooking it at a higher temperature, removing any extra fat ahead of time will result in a much leaner and more tender meat with a lot better texture.

For meat and poultry, most people prefer to leave the bones in for added flavor. Removing the bones from fish is best done ahead of time though.

Shaping and Portioning Food

It's normally helpful to cut your food in to the portions and shapes you will serve it in before you bag and cook it. This makes finishing the food much quicker and ensures that you are portioning it evenly.

Some more tender foods like fish are much harder to portion once they are cooked, so doing it ahead of time is critical.

This portioning process can also really help speed up cooking times. For instance, a whole pork loin roast might take 6 to 7 hours to heat through. Cutting it in to several 1" to 2" (25mm to 50mm) slabs before bagging them in a single layer would cut this time down to around 2 hours. So unless you want the entire roast for presentation purposes, there's no reason not to cut it down ahead of time.

Salting Before Sous Vide

When cooking meat with almost any traditional cooking method the first step is to salt it. This is also true for many items cooked sous vide, but not all of them. Here's a look at whether you should salt before you sous vide.

Pre-Salting Your Red Meat

For red meat that is cooked for shorter amounts of time, less than 4 or 5 hours most people agree that it is best to salt. I always salt short-term meat using about the same amount I would when grilling or pan searing.

However, for longer cook times there is more disagreement about when you should salt your meat. Meat that is cooked for longer amounts of time that has been salted loses a little more moisture than unsalted meat. Salting the meat also subtly changes the structure of the proteins on the outside, making the meat a little tougher and more "cured" tasting.

I personally find the flavor of salted meat beefier and richer tasting. Because of this, I usually lightly salt longer cooking items, using about a quarter as much salt as I would normally. Many people prefer the unsalted, slightly moister meat so they refrain from salting until after the meat has been cooked sous vide.

The difference between the two methods is very minor and you can't go wrong either way. I suggest trying it both ways and see what you personally prefer.

Pre-Salting Your Fish

There might be disagreement about whether or not to salt your meat before sous vide but most people agree that fish benefits greatly from a pre-salting. The flesh of sous vide fish can lack a little structure, especially when cooked at lower temperatures, and pre-salting it really helps to firm up the flesh and give it some much-desired bite.

You can introduce the salt either in a typical brine (see below) or by simply salting the fish and then resting it in the refrigerator for 30 minutes or so. You can then cook it as you usually would and the benefits should be noticeable.

Brining Your Food

Traditionally it makes a ton of sense to brine your chicken, pork or fish. It can add a lot of flavor as well as keep them really juicy. With sous vide, you don't need the additional moisture for chicken or pork, so skipping the brine is often best unless it's for flavor reasons alone.

Fish, on the other hand, greatly benefits from a brine of some kind.

Seasoning Your Food Before Sous Vide

Often spices and seasoning go hand in hand with salting your food. With sous vide, even if you want to leave out the salt, it's often a good idea to add more flavors through seasonings.

Use Herbs and Spices in Sous Vide

Using herbs and spices are a great way to add flavor to food you are going to sous vide. There are several ways to do this.

Spices and Spice Rubs with Sous Vide

My favorite way to add flavor to sous vide food is through spice rubs. They are easy to make, easy to apply, and are hugely customizable. You can use dry rubs in about the same quantities as you would for a traditionally cooked dish, though it's better to err on the lighter side than the heavier side.

Fresh Herbs with Sous Vide

Fresh herbs also work great in sous vide cooking. Harder, "woody" herbs such as rosemary, thyme, bay leaves and sage can be used in any length of cooking at most temperatures. The softer, more delicate herbs can be used in low-temperature preparations or added once the food has been cooked.

Citrus

Citrus is another great way to add flavor to sous vide food. You can use either just the peel, or the peel with the flesh. This is an easy way to impart base flavors to foods, especially more mild ones like fish or pork.

Aromatics with Sous Vide

Aromatics like garlic, onion, and ginger are best to skip when cooking sous vide. The lower temperatures used often do not cut the flavor of the aromatics the way traditional cooking does. This results in sharp, cutting flavors, not the complex flavors you are used to.

Use Sauces with Sous Vide

Sauces are a great way to add flavor to sous vide. The sauce will add flavor and somewhat permeate the food, similar to a flavor-based marinade.

This technique can be used to add strong flavors to the food. Using several tablespoons of BBQ sauce, hot sauce, teriyaki sauce, and other strong sauces is a great way to ensure the flavors transfer to the food.

Base flavors can also be introduced this way. I'll often use a tablespoon of soy sauce, Worcestershire sauce, liquid smoke, or other strong condiment to add base flavors to foods.

It's best to skip sauces that are high in alcohol or vinegar because they will not boil off.

Marinating with Sous Vide

Marinades are traditionally a great way to add flavor to meats, they also often help tenderize and break down the proteins in the food. While the tenderization is no longer needed with sous vide, the addition of the flavor is huge.

The best way to approach marinating with sous vide is to treat it like you usually would. Make the marinade and marinate the food like normal. Remove the excess marinade, put the meat in the sous vide bag and cook it. It should turn out great and keep a lot of the flavor from the marinade.

Some people also put a little of the marinade in the sous vide bag for additional flavor. This can add some flavor, but it's best not to try and marinate while the food is actually cooking. There's a whole lot that goes in to that discussion and if you are interested you can read about it on my blog post: *Can You Marinate Food While it is Sous Viding?*[12]

Smoking Before Sous Vide

Smoking food is a great way to add additional flavor and it can easily be used in conjunction with sous vide.

Just remember that you are adding smoke flavor to the food, not replacing a traditionally smoked food. These methods will work great if you want to add some great flavor to your food, though it's still best to smoke it in a traditional manner if you want super-smokey meat with a red smoke ring.

A key point to remember during smoking is to make sure the temperature of the food stays below the temperature you will be sous viding it at. Otherwise the benefits of the sous vide process will be largely negated.

There are several good ways to keep the temperature down. The first is to use a cold smoker. Either a more professional setup or something like the PolyScience Smoking Gun. These methods only heat the food a minimal amount, if any. The Smoking Gun is usually better suited to post-sous vide smoking for a touch of aroma but it works well with more tender proteins such as fish.

The other way to keep the temperature down is to only smoke the food briefly. Because most smoking occurs around 200°F (93°C) you can usually smoke the food for at least 15 to 30 minutes before cooking it sous vide, especially if you start the smoking process with the meat taken directly from the refrigerator and use a larger cut of meat.

Using high quality liquid smoke is another way of adding a smoky flavor to your foods. When I'm in a hurry I'll often put some directly in the bag before sealing it. It can't replace traditionally smoked foods but it's great in a pinch!

ASK JASON: Should You Pre-Sear?

"Some people say you need to pre-sear your food before you cook them sous vide. Other people say to sear afterwards. Some say to do both. What's the right answer?"–Harold

It's common knowledge that sous vide foods need a sear after cooking to crisp up the exterior and add the wonderful Maillard reaction. However, whether or not to sear before sous vide is a semi-controversial question.

Many people say you should pre-sear your food before you sous vide it. This definitely speeds up the final searing process and can kill surface bacteria, but in general there is no consensus on whether or not this adds flavor.

So the decision to pre-sear or not really comes down to what you are trying to accomplish.

Pre-Sear to Sanitize the Meat

An undisputed benefit of pre-searing food is to sanitize the outside of the meat. A quick sear will kill any bacteria present on the surface. This searing is much more useful for items with longer cooking times where there may be time for bacterial growth.

Though another probably more effective way to do this is to dip the meat in boiling water for a few seconds before bagging the food.

Pre-Sear to Speed Up Browning

Pre-searing also helps the food brown more quickly during the post-sear, though the post-searing time usually isn't too large to begin with. It can help with finicky foods that have a habit of overcooking during the sear, such as thinner steaks.

Pre-Sear to Add Flavor?

Some people feel that doing a pre-sear of the meat will also help flavor it and allow the seared flavors to penetrate the meat during the cooking time. Other people feel that the pre-sear flavors do not penetrate the meat or add any additional flavors, making the additional step irrelevant to the final outcome.

There is no consensus on this issue, Modernist Cuisine and Serious Eats both say not to pre-sear while Chef Steps and The French Culinary Institute both recommend it. However, with the large amount of people looking in to the issue and experimenting with it, I think it's pretty clear that the flavor benefits, if there are any, are very minimal.

If you work in a Michelin starred restaurant where this minor flavor change is important, then running your own blind taste tests makes a lot of sense. For the rest of us cooks, doing a pre-sear probably won't make a noticeable difference, so feel free to skip the step, unless you are trying to pasteurize the surface. And if you feel strongly that the pre-sear makes a flavor difference and don't mind the extra step, by all means, give it a pre-sear!

Hopefully you understand the reasons to sear pre- and post-sous vide!

Ask Jason: Should You Pre-Boil Meat?

"Some sous vide recipes say you should boil your meat before you seal it, what is that about? I thought the point of sous viding it was to keep it at a lower temperature, definitely not boiling it. I heard it has something to do with killing bacteria, but doesn't sous vide do that anyway?" –Jackson

There's a few different things going on here and I'll try to address them all.

The boiling is usually done to kill "lactobacillus", a type of bacteria that actually thrives in the lower temperature range of sous vide cooking. This bacteria isn't harmful to you, it's actually the same kind that is used a lot when making cheese and yogurt. However, it does tend to smell bad, so your food can have a funky or "bad cheese" smell to it. It can also cause your bag to puff up which can affect the transfer of heat.

These bacteria usually only become a problem with longer cooks, those over at least 12 hours, or for some people over 24 hours. While the bacteria might be present during shorter cooks, they don't reproduce enough to be an issue so they are unnoticeable.

The bacteria are often present in the air already, which is how they get onto the meat. This means that some people will run in to trouble more often than others. I personally have never had a problem with lactobacillus or funky smells, but some people have to boil their meat every time or they can have issues.

Dunking the meat in boiling water, or searing it with a torch, before putting it in a sous vide bag will kill off most of the bacteria. This will give you enough leeway to make it through an extended cook without running in to trouble.

The meat only has to be in the boiling water for a short amount of time, most people do it for 15 seconds to 60 seconds. With that short of a time the meat will only be cooked on the extreme outside, which is a part you will probably be searing at the end anyway. The interior of the meat will be just fine and will not go above your sous vide temperatures.

So if you are having trouble with bags super-inflating or stinky meat, then maybe dipping the meat in boiling water first will solve your problem, especially on longer cooks. If you haven't run in to this issue, then it's probably safe to ignore the pre-sous vide boil. I hope this clears up why and when to boil your meat before sous vide!

How to Seal Food

There are so many options for sealing your food that it can get confusing figuring out exactly what you need. There are several ways of doing it, ranging from large chambered vacuum sealers costing over a thousand dollars all the way down to Ziploc bags from the grocery store. Here's the low down on what you'll need to master the art of sealing your sous vide food.

What Does Sealing Actually Do?

Since sous vide means "under vacuum" people understandably believe the vacuum sealing process is critical to sous vide. However, this actually isn't the case at all. With a few minor exceptions, getting an actual vacuum seal isn't nearly as important to the sous vide process as simply removing most of the air. There are a few things accomplished by sealing the food as well as by removing the air.

Keeping the Flavors In
You don't want the food directly in the water or the water leaking into the sous vide pouches. Sealing the food traps all the juices and flavor in the bags instead of losing it to the water bath.

Preventing Bags From Floating
Bags with air in them float, leaving parts of the food out of the water and potentially at dangerous temperatures. The more air you pull out, the less chance of floating you will have.

Air Transmits Heat Poorly
Air is a really poor transmitter of heat compared to water (you can stick your hand in a 400°F (200°C) oven for a few seconds but sticking it in much cooler boiling water will scald you almost instantly). So removing all the air from the sous vide pouch will result in a faster and more evenly cooked food.

Increased Holding Time
The biggest advantage vacuum sealing has over other types of sealing is that you can store the food for a longer time before and after cooking it. This is especially helpful in restaurants but usually doesn't come in to play for most home kitchens.

Types of Sous Vide Sealers

Here are the most popular methods of sealing food for sous vide cooking. There are also links and descriptions of these items in the Equipment Links chapter.

Chambered Vacuum Sealers

This is the best, but most expensive, method of sealing food for sous vide cooking. Chambered vacuum sealers are large devices that can suck the air out even if there are liquids in the bag. They usually have a variable vacuum strength you can set which is great for other modernist techniques like compression and infusing. The cost of bags is also pretty small for chambered sealers, running about $0.14 per bag.

However, chambered vacuum sealers do come with downsides. They tend to run at least $500 and up to more than $1000. They are also big and heavy, most weigh between 50 and 85 pounds (22 to 39 kilograms) which makes them hard to move from the counter top.

The most consistently highly rated chambered vacuum sealers are the VacMaster brand sealers. The two most common models are the VacMaster VP210 and the less powerful VacMaster VP112. Most of their models are highly regarded. We also did an in-depth review of the PolyScience 300 Series Vacuum Sealer[13].

FoodSaver-Type Edge Sealers

Edge sealers are a good intermediate step if you want the power of a vacuum seal but don't want the bulk or expense of a chambered vacuum sealer. They are much less expensive, usually around $100 to $200 and are small and portable. They are also great if you pre-package a lot of food at home since they help food last a lot longer in the freezer without getting freezer burn.

The largest downside to edge sealers is that they can't effectively seal bags with liquids in them. The pump will pull the liquids out with the air, preventing the bag from sealing well. Edge sealers also can't pull too much of a vacuum compared to chambered sealers and are usually not adjustable.

The bags themselves are also very expensive, usually about $0.75 per bag, or 5 times what a chambered sealer or Ziploc bag costs. I know several people who prefer Ziploc bags and set aside the $0.50 difference every time towards saving up for a chambered vacuum sealer.

The most common brand of edge sealer is the FoodSaver. Both the FoodSaver V2244 and FoodSaver V3240 models are highly regarded. I've also been using the smaller Oliso vacuum sealer as well, which fits much better in my small NYC apartment.

Ziploc Bags

Many people are surprised when I tell them that the type of sous vide pouch I use most often is standard Ziploc Freezer Bags, usually in the gallon size. They are inexpensive, easy to find, and very easy to use. They get almost as good of a seal as the edge sealers if you use the water displacement method.

Ziploc bags also handle liquids better than edge sealers so you can use sauces and marinades in your sous viding. And of course, the upfront cost of $5 for a box of Ziplocs to try it out is hard to beat!

Another thing I really like about using Ziploc bags is that they are easy to open and reseal. Many foods like sirloin, brisket, and pork shoulder have a lot of variety in the toughness of the meat and need different lengths of cooking time, which can be hard to determine before actually cooking them.

With Ziplocs I can open the pouch after the minimum amount of cooking time has passed and check the tenderness. If it needs more tenderizing I just reseal the bag and put it back in the sous vide machine for a few more hours. When it's tender enough, I'll pull it out and it's ready to serve whenever I want. It really helps prevent under- and over-cooking foods.

Opening and resealing the bags is also helpful if the food has given off some gas and is starting to float. This often happens during longer cooks and it can be a pain to try and weigh down the bags. With Ziplocs, you can release the gas, reseal the bag, and the food will easily stay below the water again.

The downside to Ziploc bags is the occasional leakage of water, especially for longer cooks at higher temperatures. If I'm cooking for longer than a day I'll often use my FoodSaver or at least double bag the food.

Other Containers

Depending on the type of food you are cooking you can also use high-quality plastic wrap, Mason jars, oven bags, and ceramic ramekins.

There are also hand pump bags, sous vide-specific "zip-top" bags, and other miscellaneous sealers. But I've found that unless you're doing something specific (ramekins work great for custards, plastic wrap is wonderful for roulades, etc.) either a chambered sealer, edge sealer, or Ziploc bag works best.

Water Displacement Method

The best way to remove all the air from Ziploc bags is to use the water displacement method. Once you get the process down it is quick and easy to do.

You start by placing your food in the bag, including any liquids or marinades. Another benefit of the water displacement method is that it works equally well on dry food or liquids.

Once the food is in the bag you seal all but one corner of the Ziploc.

Place the bag in the water bath, being sure everything below the zip-line is covered by water. You can see how all the air is forced out of the pouch.

Once the air has all been removed, seal the rest of the bag.

Water Displacement Method Tips
I try to seal the food before the water has heated up but if the water is hot you can use a wooden spoon to hold the bag under while you remove the air.

I almost always use the gallon size Ziplocs. I find the extra room at the top makes them much easier to seal. The larger size also makes it easier to keep the food under the water while the top of the bag sticks out.

How to Prevent Sous Vide Bags from Floating

One of the frustrating issues people can run into is floating sous vide bags. There are several things that can cause this floating, with the most common being an excess of air in the bag. Another cause is buoyant food such as frozen chicken or several types of vegetables.

In addition to being a hassle, floating bags can also be dangerous since any of the food that is out of the water will not be held at the proper temperature. This can potentially result in unsafe conditions and bacterial growth.

The amount of floating can range greatly. Some bags might barely raise to the top of the water bath while some may fill completely with air and be so buoyant they push the top of your container off.

There are several ways you can combat the floating and some are more effective than others depending on what is causing it.

Get All the Air Out

If your sous vide bags are floating due to air in them, the easiest way to fix it is simply to remove all the air. This can entail mastering the water displacement method for Ziploc bags, getting a FoodSaver-type sealer or even a chambered vacuum sealer.

While removing the air upfront is the easiest solution, not everyone can afford a great vacuum sealer. Also, some meat and vegetables are really hard to work with, even with the higher-end sealers. In addition, many fruits and vegetables put out gases as they are cooking, regardless of how well the air was removed initially.

So here are a few more tricks and tips you can use to prevent your bags from floating.

Clip the Bags Up

If you are dealing with a bag that is just floating a little bit, you can often secure the top in place with a clip of some kind. This will prevent it from moving around too much and floating to the top. I usually use alligator clips or potato chip bag clips.

This is especially effective if you make your sous vide pouch large enough that the food can be at the bottom of the container while the bag stretches from the top to the bottom. This will give it a little more stability and help prevent floating. It will also give you a little more room at the top of the bag for the air to accumulate without affecting the food below it.

These clips also work well in conjunction with some of the other techniques I'll mention below, since they are easy to use to attach the sous vide bags to the side of the container or other items.

Open and Reseal Your Bags

One option is to periodically open your sous vide bag, let the air out, and then reseal the bag. This trick works great when gas is being released during the cook, such as with certain vegetables or frozen foods. It is also much easier if you are using Ziploc bags since they are designed to be opened and closed.

If you are using vacuum sealed bags, you can often make them longer than normal, giving you more room to work with when resealing. However, you want to be very careful not to suck up any juices that might have been released in the bag.

Weight Down Your Bags

Another solution for sous vide bags that are trying to float is to weight them down. The extra weight will counteract the buoyancy of the air or food and help hold the bag in place.

There are many options for weighting down a bag, including:

- Put a few heavy butter knifes in the bag with the food
- Pie weights
- Pennies or nickels
- Use fishing weights, though make sure they are stainless steel and not lead
- Glass bead or marbles
- Whiskey Stones

When using the weights, many people suggest just placing them in the bag with the food. However, I and many other people feel it's best to separately seal the weights, then place the sealed bag in with the food or simply attach it to the outside of the sous vide food bag with a clip or cling wrap.

Sealing the weights separately will ensure that no flavor is transferred between the items. It also means you are 100% certain no harmful chemicals leach out of the weights. Not to mention that cleanup is a lot easier if your weights haven't been simmering in meat juice for hours!

Use Magnets to Hold Bags in Place

A favorite method I had read about and have been experimenting with is to hold the bags in place with magnets.

You can place one magnet on the outside of the water bath and either a magnet or piece of metal on the inside of the water bath that is attached to the sous vide bag. It's usually best to have the item on the inside not be in the pouch with the food, as some metals can transmit flavors and might not be food safe.

If you are using a metal pot, you can just use a magnet on the inside of the water bath and it should work just fine.

Some magnets can't be heated though, so make sure the one you get can withstand the temperatures used in cooking.

I also highly recommend sealing the magnets separately from your food as they are often not food safe.

Even though I'm still experimenting, I've have good success using two bar magnets, a few disc magnets, and even a clip magnet, not to mention some sous vide-specific magnets.

Use Racks to Hold Bags in Place

Many people have sous vide racks or use covers on the water bath to help hold down floating bags. When the bags are just lightly floating, often times the added friction and placement of racks can help hold them down.

When it comes to racks, there are many options including:

- Professional LIPAVI racks
- Sous Vide Supreme rack
- Ikea dish rack
- Other sous vide racks

Racks are also great when you have multiple bags in the water bath and you want them to stay in place and not bunch up. This aids in circulation and even heating of the items, which is very important with multiple bags. The racks can also be used with the other options discussed including weighting down the bags and leaving the tops open.

If you just can't get the food to stay in the rack, you can always tie it on with butcher's string or silicon ties. Make sure you only tie a sous vide bag to something like a rack that the water can easily circulate through.

Kitchen Items as Barriers

Other people who have not purchased racks yet also have some inventive solutions to holding the bags in place.

To simulate a rack, some food people will use stainless steel strainers or flexible stainless steamer baskets. It's also often possible to wedge a large metal serving spoon above the bag.

Some people force the bag in place using a variety of items. Many use a heavy ceramic plate or bowl to hold the bag in place. Others use their metal pot lids. Glasses and mugs are also sunk next to the bags to prevent them from moving.

A few people even just stick a brick ino the water, though I'm not sure how well it would hold up over time!

Don't Seal Your Bag

If your bag is filled with air and clipping or weighting it down doesn't work, you often need to take more drastic measures.

The physics behind the water displacement method ensure that all the air is pushed to the top of the bag but it will then often cause the bags to float once too much of it accumulates. This happens both with Ziploc bags and vacuum sealed ones.

If this regularly becomes an issue for you with certain types of food you can simply leave the bag unsealed. Make sure that the sous vide bag is long enough to reach above the water line where you can clip it in place. The pressure of the water will prevent air from entering the bag while the pressure of escaping air can force its way out.

You can still seal most of the bag if you want, leaving just a corner open, or using a knife to cut a small hole in an already sealed bag. Be sure the opening is out of the water though. Also, make sure that if you do this, that the food itself stays below the water line at all times.

How Much Food Can I Put in a Bag?

People are often curious how much food they can put in to a single sous vide bag. There's a few ways to answer this question and I want to look at them in more depth.

Does the Amount of Food Affect the Cook Time?

With the power of today's sous vide circulators, the amount of food you put in a sous vide bath doesn't matter, as long as it isn't so full that the water can't circulate between the items. So you can cook 1 chicken breast in the same amount of time as 12 chicken breasts, as long as there is room between them for ample circulation.

Stacking the breasts, or having the bags too close together, effectively increases the thickness of the chicken and will require longer cooking times. So the answer to "How does the amount of food I add to sous vide affect the cook time?" is that it doesn't, as long as the water can circulate.

How Much Food Can Go In One Bag?

Most sous vide recipes will say something along the lines of "Place the chicken breasts in a sous vide bag then seal". The food should actually be in a single layer and not just piled in, though many recipes don't clarify this. I've seen multiple people not realize it should be in a single layer and they end up stacking their food in the pouches.

What's the biggest issue with this? Sous vide cooking times all depend on the thickness of the food. So if you follow a recipe for chicken breasts, it might tell you to cook it for 2 to 3 hours, which is long enough to pasteurize a 1.5" to 2" chicken breast (40mm to 55mm) when cooked at 145°F (63°C).

This is true regardless of how many chicken breasts you are cooking, as long as the thickness is within that range. However, if your chicken breasts are next to each other in the sous vide bag, the actual thickness is double or triple what the recipe called for and the innermost chicken breast will not be fully cooked, leading to potential safety issues.

So the general answer to "How much food can go in to one bag?" is as much as you can fit in a single layer. It is also imperative that all the items in the bag can be completely submerged in the water bath.

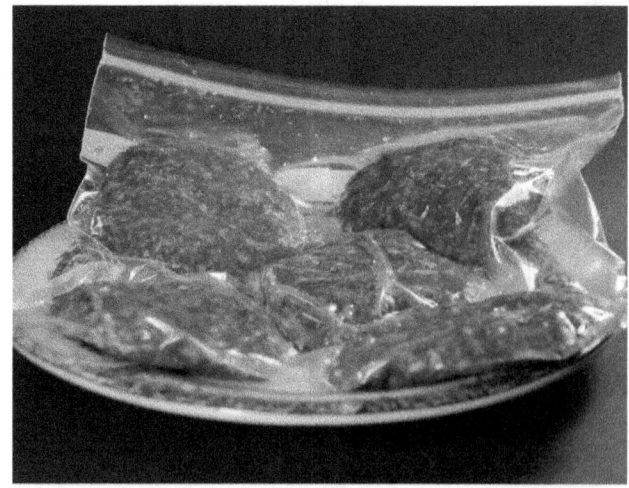

Ask Jason: Sous Vide in Store Packaging?

"Both my butcher and grocery store regularly sell meat that is prepackaged in cryovac packages, is it safe to sous vide these store bought packages? Or do I need to repackaged them before cooking? It seems like it would work fine but I wasn't sure." –James

A lot of food these days is sold in sealed packages and people always want to know if they can just put the whole package in their water bath or if they need to re-bag it. It makes sense because the allure of buying some pre-sealed meat, placing it directly in the sous vide machine, and having a great meal is so enticing. Unfortunately, as with most common questions, the answer really is "It depends".

This is mainly because when we talk about prepackaged foods there is a really wide range of types of meat and types of packaging used. These can range from high quality beef your local butcher vacuum seals for you, to cheap flimsily-wrapped chicken bought in bulk, or even marinated and seasoned meats. Depending on what type of packaging and meats you are using there's a wide range of safety and flavor information.

There are three main questions we will look at: 1) Will the store-sealed bags stay sealed, 2) Is it safe to sous vide in store packaged bags, and 3) Will there be flavor loss from store cryobags.

Note: I'll discuss all three questions and show that there are often many times you can cook directly in that packaging. However, I almost always repackaged my meat before cooking it unless I fully trust the packaging it came in. I tend to err on the side of safety, especially since it's often only a minor gain in convenience. Repackaging also allows me to season the food.

Will They Stay Sealed for Sous Vide?

No one wants their bag to come apart and leak juices in their sous vide machine but luckily this is perhaps the easiest question to answer.

The two general types of packaging used by stores are heat-sealed and glued. Heat sealed packaging will not leak unless there is a hole in the bag or it has a bad seal. Glued packaging will almost always leak or even come fully apart.

How to Tell the Difference

There are a few ways to tell if prepackaged meat is heat-sealed or glued.

Many packages are designed so you can peel off the packaging and easily remove the meat from inside. These are almost always glued.

Most heat-sealed packages will have a rough pattern where the seal is, often a zigzag or crosshatch pattern where the two sides were melted together.

If you are unsure of the type of bag, it's usually best to stay on the safe side and re-bag it.

Is it Safe for Sous Vide?

This is a much more difficult question to answer than whether or not the bags will leak. The biggest issue in sous vide safety when using pre-packed bags is determining what type of plastic is being used.

There are various kinds of plastic bags, some are not food safe at all, some are food safe only at low temperatures, and some are food safe even at or above boiling. Sous vide should always be done in bags that are food safe up through boiling (or at least the temperature you plan to cook your food at).

The concern with non-food-safe bags is the leaching of chemicals into your food. Not only is this unsafe, potentially leading to cancers and other issues, but it is also invisible. This means that you will not see any immediate issues when cooking with unsafe bags.

ChefSteps had a nice write-up about this subject in their *Is Sous Vide Plastic Safe?*[14] article. The USDA[15] also has a nice look at various types of packaging and general packaging issues.

If you are sure the store is using high-quality, food-grade plastic rated for high heat, then they should be just fine. Otherwise it's normally best to re-bag the food yourself.

How to Tell the Type of Plastic

It is often hard to tell what type of plastic food is packaged in but there are a few things you can check to try and get an idea.

Ask Them

The easiest way is to contact the store you bought it from, or the company that produces it. Just send them an email, or call them, and ask what type of plastic they use in their packaging. You can also ask if it is rated for low-temperature cooking temperatures.

Asking about the type of plastic is obviously easier if you are dealing with a local butcher or small store you frequent often but sometimes large companies will still get back to you. For instance, someone wrote to Foster Farms Chicken to ask if they could cook in their bags and got this in response:

"Thank you for taking the time to contact our Foster Farms Consumer Affairs Department. The chicken is not meant to be cooked in the packaging, it is not safe."

Getting the information directly from the company is often your best bet.

Look for "Microwave-Safe"

If packaging is labeled as "microwave-safe" or "boil-safe" it is usually fine to use with sous vide.

Check for Plastic Codes

Many plastic containers have codes on the bottom indicating what type of plastic they are made from. Recycling New Jersey[16] explains how to find them and what they mean, as does io9[17]. For those in the UK, here is a list from CS Recycling[18], though I believe they are international symbols and should be the same.

When All Else Fails

My general rule of thumb is to assume the store used the cheapest packaging they could get away with. If I don't know what type of plastic it is I always just take the five minutes and repackage the food in my own sous vide bag to be safe.

Other Safety Issues

There are a few other minor safety issues to be aware of.

Absorbent Pads and Inserts

Another safety issue with sous viding directly in store packaging is missing other things that are in the package. Some packages of meat contain absorbent pads on the bottom. These pads are often obscured by the meat and packaging, and they are almost never rated for cooking temperatures.

Some packages also contain small pouches of spices or preservatives, wax paper, or other inserts, all of which are rarely safe to heat.

Watch Those Labels

While not a safety issue, be aware that placing packaging in your sous vide water bath will usually strip off all the labels from it. These can get caught up in your sous vide machine and should be removed before cooking.

Stacked Meats

Some prepackaged meats come stacked on top of each other in the container, multiple racks of ribs are a very common example of this. If you leave them stacked, you need to be sure you extend the cook time long enough to penetrate the additional thickness of all the layers.

Will There Be Flavor Loss?

There are a few variables to consider when thinking about how flavor will be affected by cooking directly in the store packages.

Raw, Unseasoned Food

Many prepackaged foods are simply raw, unseasoned meat. When you are sous viding these in the bag they came in from the store there will definitely be some flavor loss. Or more precisely, there is no way to add additional flavor to them.

This is because usually you would want to season your meat before cooking it. This can mean spice rubs, herbs in the sous vide bag, or simply salt and pepper. If you never open the pouch, you can't add those flavors to it.

While it does result in slightly less flavorful food, I know many people have found that the trade-off is acceptable for the ability to add the package directly to the water bath.

Marinated and Seasoned Foods

Many prepackaged meats come in marinated or pre-seasoned packages. These will have no flavor loss if they are cooked directly. Most of the time these types of meats are packaged so you just cook them directly anyway.

Just make sure that the standard directions don't instruct you to wash off the marinade before cooking. This is usually true for very salty marinades and brines, such as those used with corned beef.

Some meats that are meant to be normally braised will also be overly salty to compensate for being cooked in water and might not turn out well through sous vide.

Cheap Plastic Can Smell

If cheap, unsafe plastic is used then there can also be leaching of flavor and aroma into the food...definitely not something you want!

Trimming and Cleaning

Similar to not being able to season prepackaged foods, you also can't trim and clean the food. Many cuts of meat do best with some prep work before you cook them, such as removing the membrane from ribs or the silver skin from pork tenderloin.

If you don't open the package you can't really trim and clean the meat until after it has been cooked. For most cuts this isn't a big deal, but it's something to keep in mind if you are working with food that traditionally needs some trimming before you cook it.

Hopefully now you can make the decision about whether or not to sous vide directly in the packaging from the store.

How to Sear Food

One of the areas sous vide falls short is creating that nice flavorful, brown crust on foods. Luckily there are several ways to finish off foods after they have been sous vided to create the crust without further cooking the food.

The whole goal of post-sous vide browning is to create the crust while heating the interior of the food as little as possible. The main keys to accomplishing this goal are dry foods, high temperatures, and short times.

Prepping Food for Searing

The most important thing to do before searing is to thoroughly dry it off. Moisture on the surface of the food will prevent it from browning, increasing the cooking time needed, and potentially heating the food further. Properly drying the food after sous viding is critical but easy.

Always Dry it Off
After you take the food out of the pouches pat it dry, either with paper towels or clean kitchen towels. I have a certain set of smaller towels that I only use to dry off food after sous vide, but paper towels will work well. I tend to dry it off at least 15 minutes before searing it, allowing the remaining moisture to evaporate and the meat to cool slightly.

Add a Coating
For some preparations you can add a coating to the meat before searing it as well. A light dusting of flour or corn meal will help create a crust faster and add some good flavor. Heavier coatings are also good for specific foods like breaded or fried chicken, beef Wellington, or herb crusted steaks.

Cool the Food Off
If you want to ensure you get a deep crust without overcooking the inside of the food you can also cool the food down more before searing it. This gives you more leeway in your browning time before the temperature of the inside of the food is raised too much.

Cooling the meat can be accomplished by letting it sit out before searing it. Many people leave it in the pouch and cool it in an ice bath for 5 to 10 minutes for an even better sear.

Ways of Searing Your Food

Maintaining high temperatures and short times for your searing is critical and it all comes down to what method you are using to sear it. I have links to these items in the Equipment Links chapter.

Pan Sear or Cast Iron

Pan searing your sous vide food is the easiest method for most people. It's also especially effective if you have a heavy pan or a good cast iron pan.

The process of searing it in a pan is simple. First make sure your sous vide food is completely dry. Heat a thin film of oil in the pan over medium-high to high heat until right before it starts to smoke. Add the meat to the pan, being careful of splattering, and cook for 45 to 90 seconds per side, just until the food browns.

Grilling

If you have a high-quality grill it can be used effectively for sous vide browning.

For gas grills, make sure it is turned all the way up, close the lid and let the bars fully heat. Brush oil on the meat and place on the grill, leaving the lid open. Cook for 45 to 90 seconds per side, until it browns and grill marks form.

For charcoal grills you want the coals as hot as possible. Some people even cook directly on top of their chimney-style starter to maximize the heat. Just brush the meat with oil and place on the grill, leaving the lid open. Cook each side for 45 to 90 seconds until grill marks form.

Sous Vide Torch

A favorite method of finishing sous vide is using a torch. The torch quickly browns the outside of the foods and gives you better control than searing in a pan. It is especially good for uneven foods. A down side of using the torch is that the food can sometimes develop a discernible "torch taste", though it is not something I have personally experienced.

There are many different torches but the most recommended are the Bernzomatic TS8000BT and the Iwatani Torch. The smaller pastry-style torches usually aren't powerful enough for proper browning. For a more in-depth look at the torches available you can check out our detailed guide to sous vide torches[19].

Searzall

The Searzall is a fun addition to torches. Made by Dave Arnold from the French Culinary Institute, it's an add-on for the Bernzo TS8000 torch that helps to diffuse the flame, making it better for cooking with.

Oven

The oven is pretty effective for certain types of browning. The broiler can be used for steaks or thinner cuts and the oven itself can be turned up high to brown roasts.

One of my favorite meals is sous vided prime rib roasts. After the sous vide process I'll coat them with a garlic-herb mixture and put it in the oven set to 500°F (260°C) and let the crust brown before serving it.

Deep Frying

One method of browning that people don't think of is deep frying the food. The whole concept behind deep frying is to quickly brown the outside of foods while keeping the inside tender...and that's exactly what we're looking for in a sous vide finishing technique.

To deep fry your food, heat a pot of oil to around 375°F to 400°F (190°C to 204°C); keep the pot less than half way full or it can bubble out. Make sure your food is completely dried off then place in the oil. It should take 30 to 90 seconds to fully brown the food. Remove it from the oil and you're all set.

Ask Jason: How to Keep Sous Vide Food Hot?

"I feel like when I serve sous vide meat it is cooler. I struggle to keep it warm from the sear to the table. Any suggestions?" –Sally

This is a great question! It's definitely harder to keep sous vide food hot for as long as traditionally cooked food. This is in large part due to the temperature differences inside the meat that result from the different cooking methods.

With sous vided meat, even post sear, the temperature just below the surface isn't much above the water bath temperature, usually between 130°F to 140°F for most meats (54.5°C to 60°C). This is because the water bath keeps the temperature even and gives you the lovely, evenly cooked "edge to edge" doneness. With traditional cooking you get the "bullseye" effect, where the outside layers are much more cooked than the inside. While this layering isn't as tasty, it is much hotter and therefore keeps the rest of the meat hotter for longer.

So, how to solve it? It's pretty tough to fully replicate the heat retention of traditionally cooked food but there are two methods that will help.

Don't Let Food Rest After Searing

The easiest and most important way to ensure your food is hot is to serve it directly after searing. With traditional food we usually pull the meat off the heat and let it "rest" for 5 to 10 minutes to finish cooking, distribute the heat more evenly, and cool off some, all of which helps to keep in the juices. We use this time to finish the sides, get the plating together, and set the table.

With sous vide, this always results in lukewarm food. Sous vide is already cooked to an even temperature so there is no reason to let it "rest" like you need to do with traditionally cooked foods. The longer the food sits after the sear, the cooler it will become, so make sure all your sides and plating are done before you sear the meat.

Sous vide also makes this easy because it is so forgiving. You can leave your meat in the water bath until you are about ready to serve dinner and this will greatly help minimize the heat loss.

Sometimes I want a real strong sear and I leave my meat out of the water bath for a while so it can cool off, letting me sear it longer. If you do this, just make sure you time the sear to finish when everything else is ready to be served. This doesn't work as well with a torch because it will not usually raise the temperature of the meat that much so torching is best done right after it comes out of the water bath.

> **Note:** For a great look at the science behind resting I highly recommend this Serious Eats article: http://bit.ly/2mjOC24

Heat Your Plates

The other simple way to keep sous vide food hot is to heat up your plates. Place some oven-safe plates in your oven then set it on the lowest setting it will go. This will keep your plates hot, which will carry over and keep your food hot for much longer. Just be sure to use pot holders because the plates can get hot. If your oven doesn't go below 170°F (76°C) or so, you can let it heat up then turn it off before putting the plates in it. That way they aren't hot enough to burn people or continue cooking your food.

If your sides are done, and they are hot sides, you can even plate them before you put the dishes in the oven. That way they stay warm while you are searing the meat.

Hopefully those two methods will help you keep your sous vide meat hot until your friends and family can enjoy it!

Sous Viding in Bulk

There is a lot of focus on the gourmet benefits of sous vide, with perfectly cooked meals and high quality dishes, but often the convenience of sous vide is overlooked.

One of the biggest benefits to sous vide, and one many people don't consider, is how much it can help with bulk cooking. Using sous vide it becomes much easier to cook large amounts of food that you can then store for use later.

Benefits of Sous Viding in Bulk

There are several benefits to cooking in bulk and using sous vide makes the process that much easier.

The main benefit is that you can save money doing it. Buying family packs of meat, whole muscles, and other larger packages are often much less expensive than buying individual amounts.

Another benefit is to batch your active time. For many people the hardest part of cooking is finding the time to prepare their food. Cooking in bulk allows you to prepare large parts of several meals at once. Then when you are ready to eat it's as simple as taking a bag out of the freezer and cooking it.

The third benefit is portion control. This has several uses, such as if you are cooking for one so you can't eat a whole pork shoulder or you are trying to eat less by reducing your portion size. Taking the time to actively determine how much you want to eat ahead of time is a great way to keep your portions consistent and only cook what you need at any one time.

All of this results in a lot of convenience. Having food now ready to go in the freezer makes meal planning and last-minute meals much easier.

Bulk Sous Vide Process

There are several ways to approach cooking in bulk but the two main ones are to cook your meat then freeze it, or to freeze it raw and then cook it directly from the freezer. There are a few differences but a lot of the process is the same for both. Here's a breakdown of how you can use sous vide to help reduce your cooking time.

Buy the Meat and Portion it Out

The first step is to buy and break down your meat in to good portion sizes. For many people this simply means buying meat in bulk, like a family pack of chicken breasts or multiple steaks. However, you can often save money if you purchase an entire muscle, like a whole beef loin or ribeye that you can break down in to steaks yourself.

This step also might entail cutting the meat in to pieces. For instance, if you use your chicken as a topping for salads, you might want to cut it so it's ready to go, saving you the effort of cutting it later. If you have a large pork shoulder for pulled pork, you might want to cut it in to smaller chunks that can be eaten in one sitting. Removing fat, silver skin and other undesirable parts of the food is also done now.

Season the Meat

Before bagging the meat, you can season it. If you know what your meat will be used for, you can use a specific spice rub. Otherwise, using salt and pepper is great.

Some people have concerns about salting or seasoning their meat if they are going to freeze it before cooking it. In my experience, it'll be fine as long as you aren't using a whole lot of salt (like a dry cure).

Bag the Meat

Place one or more portions of seasoned meat in a sous vide bag. Each bag will be cooked at the same time so you want to put in as many portions as you normally want to eat at a time.

For instance, I generally cook for two people so I put two portions in each sous vide bag. A family of six might want to do 3 or 6 in a bag, assuming you can get it in one layer.

If the amount of people you cook for varies a lot, you can just put a single portion in each bag and pull out as many bags as you need when you are ready to cook them.

Remove as much of the air as possible then seal them.

Cook or Freeze the Meat

At this point, you have two options. You can either freeze the sous vide bags until later, or you can sous vide them first, and then freeze them. I refer to them as the "Freeze, Cook, Eat" process and the "Cook, Freeze, Reheat" process. Your decision about which one to use really comes down the type of food, your schedule, and how you are planning to use the food.

What Type of Food Are You Sous Viding?
At one end of the spectrum you have really tender meat, like a beef tenderloin or ribeye. These items will take just about the same amount of time to cook from raw as they would to reheat. You don't gain much by sous viding them first, especially because you want to minimize the amount of time something like tenderloin is in the water bath. Winner: Freeze, Cook, Eat.

On the other side, you have real tough cuts of meat like a chuck roast. They need to be cooked for 1 to 2 days, so getting the long cook done first, then freezing them, allows you to reheat them in only an hour or two, making a quick chuck roast or pulled pork dinner very possible, even at the last minute. Winner: Cook, Freeze, Reheat.

What Is Your Schedule?
Other items depend much more on how you generally cook. Chicken breasts need to be pasteurized before you eat them, so sous viding them first will cut your reheat time by an hour or two, which might make a big difference to you. Other people have more flexible schedules so the time difference might not matter.

Flank steak or sirloin often benefits from an 8 to 12 hour cook, so Cook, Freeze, Reheat would make the reheat time much quicker. However, if you work a regular job, then the 8 to 12 hour cooking time might work better for you because you could toss it in when you leave for work in the morning. In which case, you might want to freeze it raw.

How Do You Use the Food?
How you are planning to use the food can make a big difference.

If you are using chicken to put on salads, you probably want to cook it first so you can just defrost it and toss it on the salad, even if you are at work. If it is a steak that you will be eating on the weekends using the grill, you probably have much more time to cook it the day you are going to eat it.

So depending on those factors you will want to choose the method that will work best for you.

Freeze, Cook, Eat Method

The Freeze, Cook, Eat method of sous vide is a great way to have all your meat ready to cook at a moment's notice.

Freeze Your Food

Freezing your food is easy once it is portioned and sealed in sous vide bags. Just place the bags in the freezer, preferably in a single layer, and they should be fine. The quicker you can freeze your food, the higher the end quality will be, so some people use an ice bath to quickly lower the temperature of the food before placing them in the freezer.

Cook Your Food

When you are ready to cook your food, you have two options. The first is to defrost the food in the refrigerator, then use the normal sous vide time and temperatures.

The second option is to put the frozen food directly in the water bath. This will generally increase the time needed to bring the center up to temperature by about 50%. For a tender cut this can make a big difference, a 1.5" (40mm) steak would need an extra hour of cooking time. For tough cuts, the extra hour to come to temperature is negligible compared to the 1 to 2 days you are cooking it.

Pasteurized foods are somewhere in the middle, since once they come up to temperature they need to be held there. For a regular chicken breast around 0.5" to 1.5" thick (15mm to 40mm) I will usually add an hour to the cook time. For real thick breasts I might add 2 hours and for real thin breasts maybe just 20 minutes.

Eat Your Food

Once it's cooked, finish preparing your meat like normal with a sear and then enjoy it!

Cook, Freeze, Reheat Method

The Cook, Freeze, Reheat method of sous vide is a great way to save time when you are ready to eat.

Cook Your Food

The cooking part of this method is simple. Just sous vide the food like you would if you were going to eat it right away. After it's done cooking just leave it in the pouch instead of searing it.

Freeze Your Food

If you are going to freeze food that has been sous vided, there are few steps you need to take to ensure your safety and maximize the quality of your food.

The first step is to use an ice bath to chill your food as soon as it is done cooking. Take a large bowl and fill it with ½ ice and ½ water. Take the bag from the water bath and place it in the ice bath. The length of time you will leave it depends on the thickness of the food, you can use my chart in the Cooking by Thickness chapter to determine how long to chill sous vide food. This will minimize the amount of time the food is in the danger zone and will increase its storage time.

Once the food is chilled, remove the bag from the ice bath and pat it dry. Place the sous vide bag in the freezer. The food should easily last months.

Reheat Your Food

When you are ready to eat your frozen, pre-cooked foods, there are several options.

Reheat Food in Sous Vide Water Bath

The easiest way I've found to reheat pre-cooked food is to just use your sous vide machine. As long as you set the temperature at or below the temperature you cooked it at (but at or above 130°F (54.5°C) please) it will not overcook it. I tend to stick with 130°F (54.5°C) regardless of what I'm cooking so I have more leeway in the sear.

You can use my chart in the Cooking by Thickness chapter to determine exactly how long to reheat food in a sous vide machine. Either the "Freezer Slab" or "Freezer Cylinder" columns will get you close for any time or meat, and even most poultry since it's already pasteurized. You can also speed up this process by letting the meat defrost in the refrigerator first.

Once it's heated through, you will usually want to sear the sous vided meat like normal.

Defrost Then Sear

Another way to cook your meat is to defrost it in the refrigerator, then sear it like normal. This allows you to get a much better sear on the meat without being fearful it'll be undercooked. You still need to be careful not to overcook the food while you sear it.

Just a warning that this method usually does not work if you sear with a torch because it doesn't transfer enough heat. Using a pan, grill, or broiler should work just fine though.

Heat in Sauce

If your food is part of a heavily sauced dish or a stir fry, you can defrost the meat in the refrigerator then add it directly to the meal. Be careful you don't cook the meat too long, just enough to heat it through.

Defrost Then Serve

If your food is something that doesn't need a sear, or even heated, you can just defrost it in the refrigerator and then serve it. Chicken for salads is a great example of this.

Scheduling Sous Vide

People often talk about how to use sous vide to make fancy, gourmet food but they forget that most of the time people are using sous vide to cook meals around their busy schedules. Trying to make great food, around work, school, and activities can be intimidating but sous vide can definitely make parts of it easier.

In this chapter I want to focus on the stages of sous vide and the types of sous vide foods available. Learning about these should allow you to fit sous vide in around your hectic life.

Stages of Sous Vide

There are three distinct stages of sous vide cooking we've discussed so far. Understanding them is the key to making sous vide work around a busy schedule.

The first is the Pre-Bath Stage, which is all the prep work before you actually cook the food using sous vide. This takes you from seasoning and trimming the meat up through sealing it in the sous vide bag.

The second stage is the Cooking Stage, when the food is actually in the sous vide water bath cooking.

The third and final stage is the Finishing Stage, which is when the food is seared, sides are made, and everything is plated then served.

The thing many people forget about these stages is that they don't have to be done right after each other. There are two ways to separate the stages and both can be useful for busy cooks.

The first is to add time between the Pre-Bath Stage and the Cooking Stage. This usually means getting the food prepped ahead of time and then storing it in the refrigerator or freezer until you are ready to cook it.

The second is by adding time between the Cooking Stage and the Finishing Stage. This usually entails chilling the cooked food in an ice bath then storing it in the refrigerator or freezer until you are ready to reheat and use it.

By manipulating the 3 stages and the 2 gaps between them, you can make everyday food preparation much easier.

Types of Sous Vide Foods

For everyday cooking, there are four types of sous vide foods that work well. They are Day-Of Meats, Multi-Day Meats, Fast Cookers, and Cook, Chill, and Hold foods. Each of these types of food can fit around your schedule, and manipulating the stages will give you even greater benefits.

Day-Of Meats

Day-Of Meats are meats that are generally cooked during a typical work or errand day. This ideally means foods that are cooked for 8 to 12 hours, or however long you are generally away from home. The food is usually placed in the sous vide water bath before you leave the house, it cooks throughout the day, and then when you return you just need to make the sides, pull the cooked sous vide meat out, sear it, and then serve it.

Many people prefer to separate the Pre-Bath Stage from the Cooking Stage because they do not want to be cooking in the morning. Sous vide makes it easy to trim, season and bag the meat the night before, or even several days before and store it in the refrigerator.

Then in the morning, you simply pull the sous vide bag out of the fridge, set the water bath temperature, and put the bag in the water bath. You don't have to worry about it until you get back home.

Some people even prep a bunch of meals and freeze them, making it even easier to make meals during the week, as we covered in the previous chapter.

Best Sous Vide Day-Of Meats

Most people are out of the house for 8 to 12 hours, which means certain foods work best as Day-Of Meats. Below are some that fit well with that time range.

Beef Roasts
Prime Rib Roast: 5-10 hours
Ribeye Roast: 5-10 hours
Sirloin Roast: 5-10 hours
Stew Meat: 4-8 hours
Tri-Tip Roast: 5-10 hours

Beef Steaks
Blade Steak: 4-10 hours
Flank Steak: 2-12 hours
Flat Iron Steak: 4-10 hours
Sirloin Steak: 2-10 hours
Tri-Tip Steak: 2-10 hours

Chicken and Poultry
Shredding: 8-12 hours
Thighs and Breasts: 3-12 hours
    (best at 2 to 4 hours but ok for this long)

Pork
Pork Back Ribs: 8-10 hours at high
    temperature
Pork Chops: 3-12 hours
    (best at 3 to 6 hours but ok for this long)
Country Style Ribs: 8-12 hours
Ham Roast: 10-20 hours
Shank: 8-10 hours
Sirloin Roast: 6-12 hours

WiFi Sous Vide and Ice Baths

If you have a WiFi enabled device there is a final manipulation that can be helpful to turn quicker cooking cuts of meat in to Day-Of meats. For instance, a tenderloin might only cook for two hours. You can fill your water bath with half ice and half water and place the tenderloin in there when you leave. The ice will keep the food cold for several hours.

A few hours before you want to eat you can turn on your circulator using the WiFi capability. It will finish melting the ice, bring the water up to temperature, and cook the food.

I will dive much more deeply into this process in the How to Delay a Sous Vide Cook section of this chapter.

Multi-Day Meats

The long cooking times required in sous vide are often thought of as a negative, but around a busy schedule they can be a big help. If your food cooks for longer than 12 hours, you can usually time it to be ready when you normally eat dinner.

For instance, to have food ready at dinner time on Wednesday:

- A 24 hour cook can be started when you get home on Tuesday
- A 36 hour cook can be started before you leave Tuesday morning
- A 48 hour cook can be started when you get home on Monday

All of these options work equally well and can usually be fit in even the busiest schedules.

Once you get home you simply have to sear the meat and make the sides. It allows you to have some incredible weekday dishes with very little effort.

Similar to the Day-Of Meats, it's easy to season and bag the meat ahead of time so you only have to throw the sous vide bags in the water bath when you are ready.

Best Sous Vide Multi-Day Meats

There are a lot of types of food that have multi-day cook times, and here's a few of my favorite ones. Remember that a 2 to 3 day cook will generally be ready anytime in that range, which gives you a lot of leeway.

Beef Roasts
Bottom Round Roast: 2-3 days
Chuck Roast: 2-3 days
Pot Roast: 2-3 days
Beef Ribs: 2-3 days
Beef Shank: 2-3 days
Short Ribs: 2-3 days
Top Round Roast: 1-3 days
Beef Cheek: 2-3 days
Brisket: 2-3 days

Beef Steaks
Bottom Round Steak: 2-3 days
Chuck Steak: 1-2 days
Eye of Round Steak: 1-2 days
Flank Steak: 1-2 days
Skirt Steak: 1-2 days
Top Round Steak: 1-2 days

Lamb
Arm or Blade Chop: 18-36 hours
Breast: 20-28 hours
Leg, Bone In: 1-2 days
Leg, Boneless: 18-36 hours
Osso Buco or Shank: 1-2 days
Ribs: 22-26 hours
Shoulder: 1-2 days

Pork
Pork Belly: 2-3 days
Butt and Shoulder: 1-2 days
Pulled Pork: 1-2 days
Ribs: 12-24 hours at low temperature

Fast Cookers

Fast Cookers are generally the first type of sous vide food people prepare. They are simply things that cook really fast, usually within an hour or two.

If you are trying to eat after a busy day, you will usually want to season and bag your food ahead of time, that way you can toss the sous vide bag in the water bath as soon as you step in the house. Bagging it the day before, or several days before, allows you to get it started cooking right away.

By the time you get settled, change out of your work clothes, and make the rest of the meal, the sous vide Fast Cooker can already have been cooking for an hour or two. Because of this, I only consider food a Fast Cooker if it takes less than two hours.

Best Fast Cooker Sous Vide Foods

Here are some of my favorite foods that take less than two hours to cook. Many are based on smaller thicknesses so for specific cook times, you can check out the information in the Cooking by Thickness chapter.

Sous Vide Fish
Almost any kind of fish or shellfish is cooked for less than an hour, usually in about 30 minutes.

Sous Vide Beef
There are several types of beef you can cook in under two hours as long as you don't want to pasteurize the food. Most tender steaks such as tenderloin, ribeye, or hanger steaks that are under 1.5" thick (40mm) cook in under two hours.

Sous Vide Pork
Smaller cuts of pork such as thinner pork chops or sliced pork loin can be sous vided in under two hours.

Sous Vide Chicken
You can pasteurize chicken breasts and thighs in under two hours as long as they are thin and/or cooked above 140°F (60°C).

Fruits and Vegetables
Most sous vide fruits and sous vide vegetables are cooked for under two hours, and many for less than an hour.

Pre-Cooked Foods
Almost any type of precooked food that is under 1.5" thick (40mm) can be reheated in a water bath in under an hour or two.

Cook, Chill, and Hold

The final type of foods are those that are cooked, chilled, and then held in the refrigerator or freezer until they are ready to be reheated and used. There's a lot that can go in to this process and we covered it in much more depth in the Sous Viding in Bulk chapter.

DEEP LOOK: How to Delay a Sous Vide Cook

As more and more WiFi sous vide machines come out, many people are curious how to safely delay their sous vide cooks. There's a few ways to accomplish it and this section covers my suggestion, as well as the reasons for delaying a start.

Why Delay a Sous Vide Cook?

Many people are confused when you talk about delaying a sous vide cook. There's a few reasons to delay a cook, but the main reason is you are out of the house all day and want to cook something that only takes a few hours. Waiting until you get home to start the cooking is often very inconvenient.

For instance, if you want to cook a chicken breast, it takes about 2 to 4 hours, which is longer than you usually want to wait once you get home after a long day. If you started the sous vide machine in the morning, the chicken would cook for 8 to 10 hours and the quality of the chicken breast would be less than ideal. If you can wait to start your sous vide cook until a few hours before you are planning on getting home, then the chicken will be ready as you step through the door.

Safety Issues in Delaying a Cook

There's many options for delaying a cook, but the main concern is keeping the food safe until you start to cook it. Letting a chicken breast sit on your counter in lukewarm water is just going to get people sick. So the trick is keeping your food as cold as possible until you are ready to start cooking.

The way this is usually done is by filling your sous vide container with a mixture of ice and water. This keeps the food out of the danger zone until you remotely turn on your sous vide machine, at which point it melts the remaining ice, heats the water, and cooks the food.

We ran extensive tests[20] on how long a sous vide ice bath keeps food safe and I highly recommend you read them over to get a better feel for how different variables effect it.

The main variable to keep in mind is how insulated your container is. If you are using a cooler, or a towel wrapped container, then you have a lot more leeway (and can use a lot less ice) than a container that is not insulated.

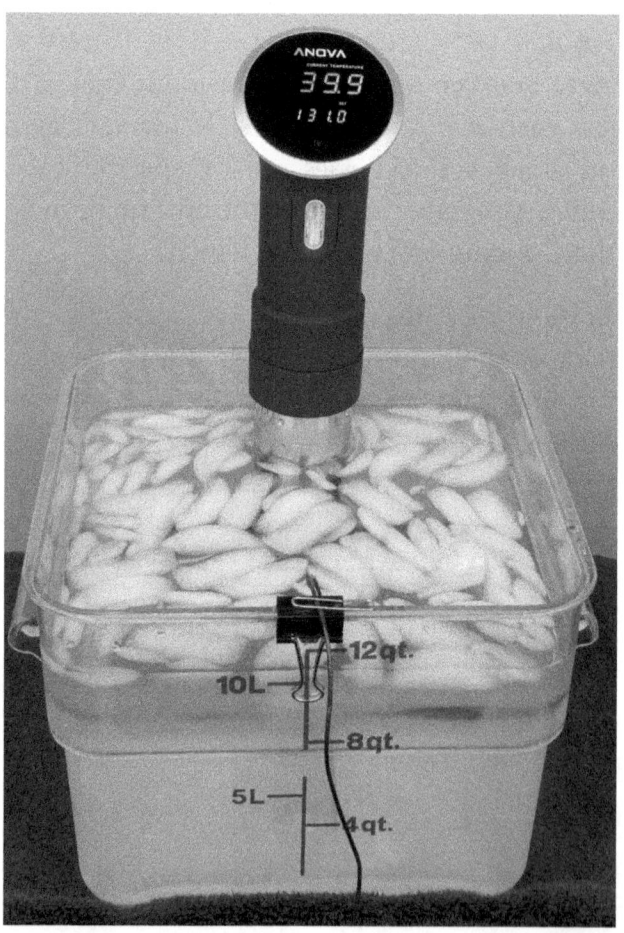

64 Amazing Food Made Easy: Exploring Sous Vide

Warning: Below is our recommended process for safely delaying a sous vide cook. But as I mentioned above, I strongly suggest you read about our ice bath experiments so you understand how your specific situation might be different. I also recommend you first test out this method with your own setup on a day you are around and can monitor the temperature yourself, just to make sure it will work for you and your specific setup.

How to Delay a Sous Vide Cook

The first step is to get an insulated sous vide water bath container. This can be as simple as wrapping a standard container in towels, or using a cooler with a hole cut in it. Using an insulted container will help it stay cold almost indefinitely and allow you to use a lot less ice. If you can't insulate your container, I recommend doubling the amount of ice suggested.

Fill your container about a third of the way full with ice then fill it with the coldest water you can get out of your tap. Another option is to refrigerate your water overnight if you have room in your fridge. This will add several hours to the amount of time the water will stay cold.

Add your food to the container. The higher the food is, the longer it will stay cold. While this sounds counter intuitive because heat rises, the ice floats so the remaining ice is always at the top, chilling that water more. In our tests, at one point the top of the water bath was 7.5°F cooler than the bottom.

Place your circulator in the water and make sure it's all set up, has power, and you can access it from your smartphone.

You are now good to go and this setup will generally keep food out of the danger zone for 10 to 15 hours.

When you want to start your cook later in the day, access your sous vide machine from your smartphone and turn it on to the temperature you want.

You will need to add some additional time to your cook to melt the remaining ice. The specific amount of time will depend on how much ice you used, how insulated your container is, how powerful your circulator is, and how long you waited before starting your cook. Generally speaking though, adding about an hour is a safe estimate.

Once you get home you can pull out your food, sear it and enjoy!

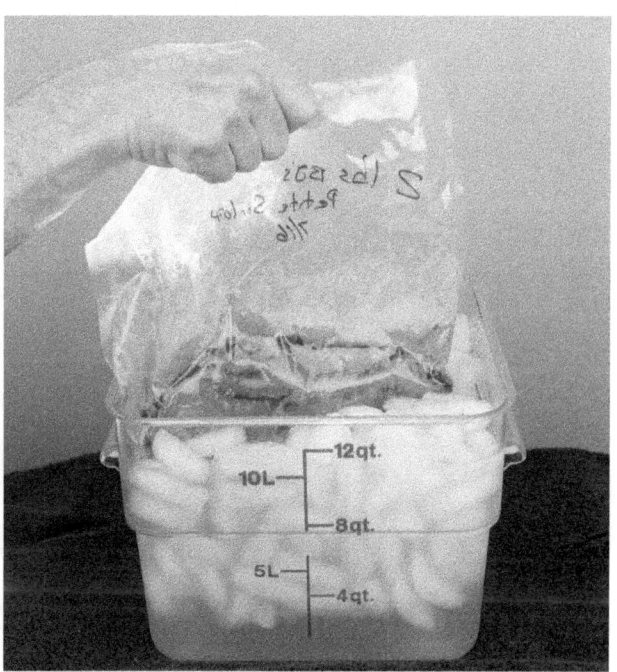

Beef and Red Meat

In previous chapters we discussed how to determine sous vide temperatures and how sous vide times work, now we are going to tie it all together and discuss how to cook beef, lamb, and other red meat.

I'll break down the various steps of cooking red meat and cover some of the time and temperatures I recommend for various cuts. I'll also give you the reasoning behind them so you can make your own decisions.

What Do I Mean by Red Meat?

Before we get to the times and temperatures, let's discuss what exactly I mean by "Red Meat". Generally, red meat refers to the meat from mammals and it all behaves pretty similarly. The ones I am most familiar with are beef, lamb, venison, and veal but I have also discussed recipes with readers who cook moose, elk, bear, kangaroo, bison, and many others. Usually pork is treated differently than red meat and we will discuss it in a future chapter.

Most red meat behaves similarly but the type of animal, and how it was raised, can lead to a few differences. Just like field-raised grass-fed cows produce meat with different cooking requirements than grain-fed feedlot-raised cows, the amount of exercise the animals get and their diet will be reflected in their meat.

Knowing that the meat generally behaves the same, you can easily apply the following times and temperatures to most types of red meat. For instance, if you have a piece of meat you normally grill to medium rare like a deer tenderloin, you can use a time and temperature for a piece of beef sous vided to medium-rare, then adjust the times as needed.

The same goes for a tough cut of meat, say a moose shoulder, that you want to shred. Just follow the time and temperature for shredded beef and you should come close.

> **Warning:** One concern is pathogens that might be present in wild game. If you are eating wild game, cooked traditionally or with sous vide, you should make yourself aware of the pathogens and what temperatures are needed to kill them as it may differ from beef.

Pre-Sous Vide Preparation

There are lots of things you can do to beef and red meat before you sous vide them. The meat is often portioned out, fat and other tough parts are removed, and the meat is shaped. It's usually then salted or a spice rub is applied. Spices, herbs, sauces, and other flavoring agents can also be added to the bag. Here's a few of my beef specific tips, but you should refer back to the Before You Sous Vide chapter for more in-depth looks at many of these hints.

Trim and Portion Your Meat

It's a great idea to remove any fat or gristle from the meat before cooking it. I often cut the meat in to portions as well. Not only does it help it cook more evenly, it can also speed up the sous vide process, especially for larger cuts of meat.

Salting Your Meat

Whether or not to salt your meat before sous viding it is a little controversial.

It is generally accepted that for short cooks, less than 4 hours or so, salting ahead of time is just fine.

For longer cooks, people tend to be split. I like to lightly salt my beef before sous viding it since I think the end result tastes more "beefy". Many people feel that the salt gives it a more "cured" flavor with a drier result. I recommend you try both and see what you prefer.

Do Not Add Fat

Adding some butter or fat to your meat seems like a good idea, and it works great for many traditional techniques. But with sous vide, the fat will actually draw the flavor out of the meat, making it blander. So leave the butter out of the bag, you can always add it at the end of the sear.

Add Rubs and Herbs

For most food cooked sous vide, using a spice rub or adding herbs to the bag is a great way to add flavors. You can use any salt-free spice rubs the way you normally would, or apply ones with salt after the meat is done cooking and before you sear it.

Marinades Are Great

Another great way to add flavor is to marinate your food. Just make sure you marinate it before cooking it, you can't really do both at the same time.

Avoid Fresh Aromatics

Unless you are cooking your meat at very high temperatures then garlic, onions, and other aromatics will not cook during the sous vide process. This means they will still have a sharp, raw flavor to them. In most cases it is best to turn to dried spices.

Add Some Smoke

Many meat preparations can benefit from some pre- or post-sous vide smoking. As long as the smoking process doesn't raise the temperature of the meat, it will have no adverse effects.

Sous Vide Temperatures for Red Meat

When you are sous viding beef or other red meats there are two main directions you can go. The first is to create a steak-like texture, and the second is to end up with a more pull-apart, braise-like texture. Regardless of the type of meat, the texture you are aiming for will determine the temperature you will use.

Steak-Like Texture

Steak-like texture is what comes to mind when you think of a typical steak. It's usually filet, ribeye, strip, sirloin, flank steak, hanger steak or another tender cut that is traditionally grilled or pan fried.

With sous vide, you can also cook tough cuts at a low temperature for an extended period of time, usually 1 to 2 days, and the result will be steak-like. This is often done with brisket, chuck roast, ribs, round and other tough cuts.

The temperatures used for steak-like texture are the easiest to determine. Most cooks, or eaters, generally know how they like their steaks, either rare, medium rare, medium or (gulp) well done. Those donenesses correspond to specific ranges of temperature, so you can have an easy starting point.

Common Tender Meat Temperatures
Rare: 120°F to 129°F (49°C to 53.8°C)
Medium Rare: 130°F to 139°F (54.4°C to 59.4°C)
Medium: 140°F to 145°F (60°C to 62.8°C)
Well Done: Above 145°F (62.8°C)

> **Warning:** Just a reminder that if you drop the temperature much below 130°F (54.4°C) you are in the danger zone, not killing any pathogens, and shouldn't cook the steak for more than a few hours.

If you are unsure of the specific temperature you like your meat cooked at in the ranges above, I recommend starting with 125°F (51.6°C) for rare, 131°F (55°C) for medium rare and 140°F (60°C) for medium. You can then adjust the temperature up or down in future cooks to better match your preference.

Traditional Braise-Like Texture

The second direction you can take red meat is in a more braise-like preparation. This is food that is similar to shredded beef, braised meats, and other "low and slow" preparations. The cuts used for this are tough and generally high in fat and connective tissue, such as chuck roast, shanks, brisket, and many other roasts.

As the food cooks at a higher temperature, the connective tissue breaks down, making the meat flaky and shreddable. The higher the temperature you use, and the longer you cook it, will cause the meat to break down more and more.

Once you've cooked meat to those temperatures you will have a better feel for the texture that results from each one. Then you can tweak the temperature and the time it is cooked to meet your standards.

> **Common Braise-Like Temperatures**
> Most braise-like temperatures range from around 150°F up to 185°F (65.6°C to 85°C).
>
> 156°F (68.8°C) for shreddable, but firm
> 165°F (73.9°C) for more fall apart
> 176°F (80.0°C) for really fall apart

Sous Vide Times for Red Meat

When you start to determine how long to cook a piece of red meat for, you first need to determine what type it is. There are broadly two types of red meat: tender cuts and tough cuts.

Tender Cuts

Tender cuts are those pieces of meat that just need to be heated through, and maybe pasteurized, before you eat them. This is usually most types of steak, tenderloins, and other cuts you would usually enjoy grilling or pan frying.

> **How Long to Heat Meat**
> In general a piece of meat will be heated through at the following rate:
>
> 0.5" (13mm) thick in 35 minutes
> 1" (25mm) thick in 70 minutes
> 1.5" (38mm) thick in 2.5 hours
> 2" (50mm) thick in 3.5 hours

You can follow the charts in the Cooking by Thickness chapter for the specific amount of time. Most red meat heats closely enough to each other for the charts to work well across most animals.

Tough Cuts

Tough cuts of meat require extended cooking times to break down and tenderize the meat. The amount of time will depend greatly on the cut. These times will usually range from 18 hours to 2 days. I have extensive time recommendations in the Cooking by Tenderness chapter.

If you are cooking a type of meat that is not covered, like elk or kangaroo, you can generally find a similar cut of beef or lamb and then start with the time recommended for it.

In-Between Cuts

Some cuts do not fall directly in to the tough or tender categories. A good example of this is flank steak or sirloin. Both cuts can be just heated through and served, but extended cooking can tenderize them slightly more, resulting in a much more tender steak. Most of these cuts can benefit from a 5 to 10 hour time in the sous vide bath.

How to Finish Red Meat

To finish red meat I will usually dry it really well, salt it and then sear it. This gives it a much more appealing look and adds a lot of great flavor.

Sear It

To sear red meat I usually pan fry it, grill it or use a torch. If I'm deep frying something else I'll often use the oil to deep fry the meat as well, which is a quick and easy way to add uniform brownness to the entire meat.

Whatever method you use, you will want to sear it very quickly to prevent it from overcooking any more than is necessary. You can also chill the meat in an ice bath for 5 to 10 minutes before searing it to give yourself more leeway.

You can read more about general searing in the How to Sear Food chapter.

Smoke It

Some people also smoke their meat after it has been sous vided, especially for brisket and other barbecued meats. It's often best to chill the meat for 5 to 10 minutes before smoking it to ensure the temperature of the meat stays low.

Ask Jason: Steaks at Different Temperatures

"My wife and I eat medium-rare steak but when my in-laws come they refuse to eat it at less than medium. How do I cook steaks to two different temperatures with one sous vide machine? I'd rather not be forced to overcook our steaks." –Jonathan

This is a pretty common question because many people don't like their steaks cooked to the same temperature. There's a few ways to accomplish this, and each one has pluses and minuses depending on the type of meat you are cooking.

The easy way is to buy another circulator!

I know, I know, that isn't practical for most people! Luckily there are other options!

Before I get started on how to accomplish sous viding at two different temperatures, I wanted to mention two things related to doneness preferences.

Safety Vs Preference

The first thing I want to remind you is that if safety is a concern, through sous vide you can fully pasteurize the food at any temperature above 130°F (54.5°C). You can use my sous vide beef, pork and lamb pasteurization times or sous vide chicken pasteurization times in the Cooking by Thickness chapter to ensure that the food is completely cooked through and safe to eat.

So if you, or the people you are serving food to, are worried about safety, you can be confident the food is safe at the lower temperature. This is doubly true for steak, since through traditional methods the inside of the steak is not pasteurized. This means that if it is blade tenderized (Costco...*cough* *cough*) there may be pathogens on the inside after it is cooked...sous vide would kill these and be safer to eat.

Give Them What They Want

On the flip side, be a good host! Some people like medium or medium-well steak. Others like dry, "over cooked" chicken. To 95% of the population, this tastes worse than properly cooked food but maybe to these people it tastes great. It's usually not worth a long discussion on why your guest is "wrong" for preferring it cooked a certain way.

I always try to provide the type of food my guests want, even if I personally think that what they want isn't as good as what I want to serve. I know I could try and explain to them that what they prefer is wrong, but everything generally goes more smoothly if I just bite the bullet and serve them what they prefer.

One caveat to this...don't feel like you need to serve them the exact same food. If you are having close friends over and cooking some awesome 60 day aged ribeye for them...but you know one of your friends only eats well-done steak then don't feel bad buying a lesser ribeye for them.

You don't have to flaunt it, or even tell them you did it, but they will probably appreciate you giving them a well-done steak more than a lecture on why they should enjoy medium-rare...and conversely you don't have to feel bad you wasted $20 on a steak you purposely burnt the crap out of.

OK, enough lectures, on with the actual answer!

To simplify the question, I'll focus on cooking two pieces of steak. The first will be cooked to medium rare at 131°F (55°C) and the second to medium at 140°F (60°C). The methods I'll discuss apply to sous vide pork, chicken, and other cuts of meat as well.

Longer Post-Sous Vide Sear Times

The easiest method to sous vide two steaks to different temperatures, and the one I use the most, is to simply sear the more well done steaks longer.

You would heat the sous vide water bath up to 131°F (55°C) and put both steaks in it. Cook both steaks until they were done, usually 2 to 4 hours for tender cuts or much longer for tough cuts.

Both steaks would be removed from the sous vide bags and dried off. You will want to sear one steak like normal, for about 30 to 60 seconds per side, so it stays at medium rare. The second steak will be seared for longer, probably 1 to 3 minutes per side, until the middle has been raised a few degrees to medium. If you have a meat thermometer you can be exact in this heating, or otherwise you can wing it, erring on the side of more- or less-rare depending on who will be eating it.

You now have one medium-rare and one medium steak, with only a few minutes of additional cooking time!

It's generally best to start with the "medium" steak first, and when it's almost done searing you can add the "medium-rare" steak for a quick sear as the first one finishes up. Also, this method works best if you are searing in a pan or a grill. Using a torch is so efficient it's hard to raise the temperature of the steak, even when you are trying to.

The biggest downside to this is that the medium steak will begin to develop more of the "bulls eye" effect that sous vide generally prevents. So if you are trying to maintain the perfect "edge to edge" doneness, it's much harder to do through this method.

Overlapping Sous Vide

The other effective way to cook food to a different temperature is to sous vide them at different times. This can be done in a few ways.

One way is to cook the medium steak first. Then turn down the temperature of the sous vide bath to medium rare and add the other steak. Because sous vide doesn't overcook the steaks, the medium one will be fine in the water bath for the extra time. Once it's cooked you can sear them both like usual. This presumes that the steaks are a tender cut like tenderloin, ribeye or strip steak and not a tough cut.

For tough cuts that cook for a long time, like a chuck steak or a flank steak, you can simply heat the medium cut through and then turn down the temperature and add the medium-rare steak for the remaining hours or days. Both steaks will tenderize over the long cook time but the medium one will still be more cooked than the medium-rare one.

The final option is the reverse of the last one. You would heat the sous vide bath to medium-rare and put both steaks in. Once the first steak is done cooking you remove it and turn the sous vide temperature up to medium. Once the second steak has come up to temperature you can take it off and sear both steaks like usual.

One benefit to this method is you can do a longer sear on the first steak because it has cooled off some. The downside is that you are adding an hour or two to your cook times.

Hopefully now you are all set to provide perfectly cooked food to all your guests!

Hanger Steak with Succotash

Cooks: 131°F (55°C) for 2 to 4 hours • Serves: 4

This recipe showcases how simple it is to cook a tender cut of steak with sous vide. I use hanger steak in this example, but it works equally well with other tender steaks such as filet, ribeye, or strip steak. Unless you are pasteurizing them, the steak only needs to be heated through because the cut is already very tender. For most cuts this will be 2 to 4 hours, depending on the thickness. You can refer to the Cooking by Thickness chapter for specifics, though going an hour or so longer will not adversely affect the meat.

In this recipe you can also use cuts of medium toughness such as sirloin or flank steak, though since they are a little tougher you can increase the time they cook for a more tender steak.

I pair it with a simple succotash, but you can use any sides you traditionally like to serve with steak.

For the Hanger Steak

2 pounds hanger steak (900 grams)

¼ teaspoon steak seasoning or chile powder

For the Succotash

Olive oil

1 red onion, diced

2 garlic cloves, minced

1 poblano pepper, diced

2 cups corn kernels

2 cups lima beans

2 tablespoons butter

1 lime

To Assemble

1 lime

Basil, chopped

For the Hanger Steak

Preheat a water bath to 131°F (55°C).

Lightly salt the hanger steak then sprinkle with the steak seasoning. Place the steak in a sous vide bag then seal the bag and cook for 2 to 4 hours.

For the Succotash

Heat some olive oil in a pan over medium-high heat. Place the red onion in the pan and cook until it starts to soften. Add the garlic and poblano pepper and cook until the poblano pepper is tender. Add the corn and lima beans and cook until the lima beans are tender. Add butter and let it melt. Juice the lime in the pan and mix well to combine.

To Assemble

Remove the cooked steak from the bag and dry the meat well. Quickly sear the steak then cut it into serving sections.

Place a few spoonfuls of succotash on a plate then top with the steak. Sprinkle some basil on top and then lightly salt.

Chuck Steak with Asparagus and Shishito Peppers

Cooks: 131°F (55°C) for 36 to 60 hours • Serves: 4

This recipe highlights how a low temperature and long cooking time can really transform a cut of meat. Compared to a traditional chuck cooked at a high temperature, this is cooked at 131°F (55°C) for 36 to 60 hours, resulting in a meltingly tender meat that tastes similar to prime rib or ribeye. You can follow this recipe for many other tough cuts of meat, such as short ribs, top and bottom round, or shank, simply adjust the timing in line with what is in the Cooking by Tenderness chapter.

For the Chuck Steak
2 pounds chuck steak or chuck roast (900 grams)
1 teaspoon garlic powder
1 teaspoon onion powder
½ teaspoon coriander

For the Asparagus
1 bunch asparagus
1 pint cherry tomatoes
Olive oil
2 teaspoons diced garlic

To Assemble
4 shishito peppers
Sage, diced
Sea salt

For the Chuck Steak
Preheat a water bath to 131°F (55°C).

If the chuck is large, cut it into 1.5" to 2" slabs (38mm to 50mm) then trim off any excess fat or connective tissue.

Combine all the spices in a bowl and mix well. Lightly coat the chuck slabs with the spices then place in a sous vide bag. Seal the bag and cook for 36 to 60 hours.

For the Asparagus
Trim the bottom off of the asparagus and cut the cherry tomatoes in half.

Heat some olive oil in a pan over medium heat. Place the asparagus and garlic in the pan and cook until the asparagus becomes tender. Add the cherry tomatoes then remove the vegetables from the heat.

To Assemble
In a hot pan, sear the shishito peppers until they just start to brown, turning until all sides get color and they begin to become tender.

Remove the cooked steak from the bag and dry the meat well. Salt the chuck and then quickly sear it. Cut the chuck into serving-sized portions.

Place a few spoonfuls of the asparagus and tomato mixture on a plate then top with the steak. Sprinkle some sage and sea salt over the dish then top with a seared shishito pepper.

Short Rib Korean Lettuce Wraps

Cooks: 131°F (55°C) for 48 to 72 hours • Serves: 4

Short ribs are a classic "must make" sous vide dish. Due to the high fat content they can be cooked anywhere from 131°F to 185°F (55°C to 85°C) for 12 hours to 3 days and the final dish will greatly depend on the time and temperature you use. The end result will range from a traditional braise-like texture to a chewy steak, or anything in between. For this recipe we want a medium-rare steak-like texture so the short ribs are cooked at 131°F (55°C) for 48 to 72 hours.

The longer the short ribs cook, the more tender they become so a 48 hour cook will be firmer than a 72 hour cook. You can follow this recipe for many other tough cuts of meat, such as chuck, top and bottom round, or shank, just adjust the timing in line with what is in the Cooking by Tenderness chapter.

I like to serve the short ribs in the Korean BBQ style with lettuce wraps, kimchi, and pickled vegetables.

For the Short Ribs
1 teaspoon salt
1 teaspoon garlic powder
½ teaspoon ginger powder
½ teaspoons ancho chile powder
¼ teaspoon chipotle chile powder
¼ teaspoon black pepper
2 pounds short ribs (900 grams)

To Assemble
Leafy lettuce, such as bibb
  or romaine
Kimchi
Pickled cucumbers
Assorted vegetables
Gochujang or other hot sauce

For the Short Ribs
Preheat a water bath to 131°F (55°C).

Combine all the spices in a bowl and mix well. Lightly coat the short ribs with the spices then place in a sous vide bag. Seal the bag then cook for 48 to 72 hours.

To Assemble
Remove the cooked short ribs from the bag and dry the meat well. Quickly sear the ribs then remove the meat from the bone and cut it into strips.

Serve everything family-style on the table, allowing people to assemble their own combination of meat, condiments, and sides on the lettuce wraps.

Smoked Brisket with Bourbon BBQ Sauce

Cooks: 150°F (65.6°C) for 18 to 36 hours • Serves: 4 to 6

BBQ brisket is traditionally smoked for several hours over low heat until the meat is fall-apart tender. I usually don't have the time to tend a brisket for that long so I turn to sous vide. I smoke the brisket for 30 to 60 minutes ahead of time, then seal it in a sous vide bag and cook it for 18 to 36 hours.

I'm looking for a more traditional brisket so I opted for 150°F (65.6°C) for 18 to 36 hours. The longer the brisket cooks, the more tender it will become so an 18 hour cook will be firmer than a 36 hour cook at the same temperature.

For the Brisket

- 2 to 3 pounds beef brisket (900 to 1360 grams)
- 1 teaspoon ancho chile powder
- 1 teaspoon smoked paprika
- 1 teaspoon dried thyme leaves
- ½ teaspoon mustard powder
- ½ teaspoon ground coriander

For the Bourbon BBQ Sauce

- 2 cups ketchup
- 1 cup Bourbon whiskey
- ½ cup brown sugar
- ½ cup water
- ¼ cup balsamic vinegar
- 3 tablespoons chopped garlic
- 1 tablespoon ancho chile powder or chile powder of your choice
- 2 tablespoons liquid smoke
- 2 tablespoons Worcestershire sauce
- ½ tablespoon chipotle chile powder or chile powder of your choice
- 1 tablespoon molasses
- 2 tablespoons whole grain mustard

To Assemble

- Arugula or other bitter greens
- Fresh parsley, chopped
- Coleslaw

For the Brisket

Prepare a smoker over the lowest heat it works at. Preheat a water bath to 150°F (65.6°C).

Mix together the spices in a bowl. Lightly salt and pepper the brisket then coat with the spices. Place the brisket in the smoker and smoke for 30 to 60 minutes, ensuring the temperature of the meat stays below the temperature you will be sous viding it at.

Once the smoking is done place the brisket in a sous vide bag and seal. Cook the brisket for 18 to 36 hours, until it is tender.

For the c BBQ Sauce

Whisk together all of the ingredients in a pot over medium-high heat and bring to a simmer. Gently simmer for at least 5 to 10 minutes, and as long as it takes to get to the consistency you prefer. The bourbon BBQ sauce will keep in the refrigerator for at least a week.

To Assemble

Remove the cooked meat from the sous vide bag and pat dry. Lightly salt the outside then quickly sear it until the meat is just browned. Cut the brisket across the grain into thin slices.

Place some arugula on a plate and top with several brisket slices. Drizzle the bourbon BBQ sauce over the top then sprinkle with the salt and parsley. Add the coleslaw then serve.

Rack of Lamb with Pomegranate and Brussels Sprouts

Cooks: 131°F (55°C) for 2 to 4 hours • Serves: 4

Rack of lamb is a rich, flavorful cut to make. Here I pair it with a zesty pomegranate sauce that cuts the richness while complimenting the strong lamb flavor. I also serve it with some Brussels sprouts to bulk out the meal while cutting the richness of the lamb. This recipe is enough for 4 if you don't need much meat, otherwise add an additional rack.

I prefer my lamb cooked to 131°F (55°C) but many people who like lamb on the more rare side drop the temperature as low as 125°F (51.6°C). Make sure not to cook it for more than 2 hours if you are below 130°F (54.4°C).

For the Rack of Lamb

1 rack of lamb, 1.5 to 2 pounds (700 to 900 grams)
¼ teaspoon coriander
⅛ teaspoon cumin
Zest from ½ orange
1 rosemary sprig

For the Pomegranate Sauce

2 cups pomegranate juice
¼ cup fresh orange juice
2 teaspoons fresh thyme leaves
1 cinnamon stick
1 ancho pepper, seeds and stem removed
1 tablespoon honey

For the Brussels Sprouts

1.5 to 2 pounds Brussels sprouts (700 to 900 grams)
Olive oil
1 shallot, thinly sliced
2 tablespoons minced garlic
2 teaspoons fresh thyme leaves
2 tablespoons water
2 teaspoons lemon zest
¼ lemon

To Assemble

Cherry tomatoes
Pomegranate seeds
Fresh oregano leaves
Smoked salt

For the Rack of Lamb

Preheat a water bath to 131°F (55°C).

Lightly salt the rack of lamb. Combine the coriander and cumin in a bowl then sprinkle over the lamb. Evenly spread the orange zest over the meat then place the lamb in a sous vide bag with the rosemary. Seal the bag and cook for 2 to 4 hours.

For the Pomegranate Sauce

Put the pomegranate juice, orange juice, thyme, ancho pepper and cinnamon in a pot over medium heat and lightly simmer for 20 to 30 minutes, until reduced and thickened. Remove from the heat, discard the cinnamon stick and ancho pepper then stir in the honey. The sauce can be made a day or two ahead of time and refrigerated, or left on the counter for an hour or two.

For the Brussels Sprouts

Cut the ends off of the Brussels sprouts and discard them. Cut the Brussels sprouts in half length-wise. Heat the olive oil in a pan over medium to medium-high heat. Add the Brussels sprouts and cook, stirring infrequently, until the Brussels sprouts start to brown.

Add the shallots, garlic, thyme, and water to the pan then cover it and let the Brussels sprouts steam until tender, 5 to 10 minutes. Remove the Brussels sprouts from the pan, toss with the lemon zest and squeeze the lemon over the top.

To Assemble

Remove the cooked rack of lamb from the bag, discarding the rosemary, and dry the meat off well. Quickly sear the lamb then cut it into serving sections, usually one or two ribs. Quickly sear the cherry tomatoes until they just burst.

Place a few sections of lamb onto the plate. Arrange the Brussels sprouts and roasted tomatoes around it. Drizzle the lamb with the pomegranate sauce. Add some pomegranate seeds and oregano leaves to the lamb, then sprinkle with some smoked salt.

Bison Strip Steak Carbonara

Cooks: 131°F (55°C) for 2 to 4 hours • Serves: 4

This recipe showcases cooking other types of red meat. I focus on bison but it would work equally well with other tender cuts of red meat such as deer or elk. Bison is becoming more and more common but is still a pretty under-utilized cut of meat. Like steak, I prefer bison cooked to 131°F (55°C) but the temperature ranges for it are similar to beef so you can adjust how you see fit.

This recipe combines the bison with a semi-traditional egg-based carbonara sauce that I bulked up with some fresh vegetables. The richness of the carbonara helps to offset some of the leanness of the bison.

For the Bison Strip Steak

1.5 to 2 pounds bison strip steak (700 to 900 grams)
1 rosemary sprig
3 thyme sprigs

For the Sautéed Vegetables

Olive oil
1 medium yellow onion, diced
1 yellow bell pepper, diced
1 red bell pepper, diced
1 small head of broccoli, cut into florets

To Assemble

Pasta, preferably whole wheat or rye-based
4 eggs
Parmesan cheese
Basil, cut into strips

For the Bison Strip Steak

Preheat a water bath to 131°F (55°C).

Lightly salt the bison then place it in a sous vide bag with the rosemary and thyme. Seal the bag and cook for 2 to 4 hours.

For the Sautéed Vegetables

Heat the olive oil over medium heat. Add the onion and cook until it begins to soften and turn translucent. Add the yellow and red bell peppers as well as the broccoli and cook until the broccoli is tender. Remove from the heat.

To Assemble

Remove the cooked bison from the bag, discarding the herbs, and dry the meat off well. Quickly sear the bison then cut it into ½" slices (25mm).

Cook the pasta until done then immediately add to individual bowls and crack an egg into each one. Stir well to ensure the egg cooks in the pasta. Grate fresh parmesan cheese into each bowl and stir well. Top with the sautéed vegetables, slices of bison, and basil. Grate some more cheese on top then serve.

Pork and Boar

In this chapter we will discuss the best way to sous vide pork and boar. In general, sous vide pork turns out much more moist and tender than it does with any other cooking technique. It's also safer to eat because you can fully pasteurize it without over cooking it.

In a previous chapter we discussed how to sous vide beef and red meat, and pork follows very similar guidelines but with generally higher temperatures on the low end. This chapter will help you make the most out of all types of pork, including supermarket pork, pastured pork, wild/semi-wild boar, and other porcine.

Most types of pork or boar behave very similarly but there are differences that can arise based on the type of animal and how it was raised. A feedlot-raised pig will taste different than a pasture-raised pig since their diet and amount of exercise will alter the flavor and texture of their meat.

Pre-Sous Vide Preparation

There are lots of things you can do to pork before you sous vide it. Any silver skin is removed as is extra fat. The meat is often cut into portions or shaped and any spice rubs or salt is added. Spices, herbs, sauces, and other flavoring agents can also be added to the bag. Sous vide pork is usually not brined since it doesn't add that much.

I'll share some of my tips for pork, but you should refer back to the Before You Sous Vide chapter for more in-depth looks at many of these ideas.

Trim and Portion Your Meat
Some cuts of pork are filled with fat, gristle, or silver skin and it is usually a good idea to trim it off and remove it ahead of time.

Cutting your pork into portions before cooking can also be beneficial. It can speed up the sous vide process for larger cuts and make the meat cook more evenly.

Skip the Brine
With many types of traditional cooking, brining the pork ahead of time is a great way to keep it moist. However, this step is generally unnecessary with sous vide, and often times will actually cause the pork to taste blander than if it was just sous vided like normal.

Add Some Smoke
Just like with beef, some smoke can be a great addition to pork. Just make sure you keep the temperature of the meat below the sous vide temperature and it should turn out great.

Sous Vide Pork Temperatures

When you are sous viding pork you are usually aiming for either a chop-like or a braised / shreddable texture. The choice of texture you want determines the temperature you will use. For more information you can go back and read the Determining Temperature chapter.

Warning: One concern is pathogens that might be present in wild animals. If you are eating wild animals, cooked with sous vide or traditionally, you should be aware of the pathogens and what temperatures are needed to kill them.

Chop-Like Texture for Pork

Chop-like texture is what you usually associate with pork chops, pork loin, or other juicy, firm preparations. Traditionally they are made from cuts that can be quickly cooked either by pan frying, roasting, or grilling.

With sous vide, you can also cook tough cuts at a low temperature for an extended period of time, usually 1 to 2 days, and the result will be chop-like. This is often done with shoulder, shank, butt, ribs and other tough cuts.

There's a range of temperatures you can use to sous vide pork, and it is safe as long as it's cooked above 130°F (54.4°C), but most people prefer their pork cooked higher than 135°F (57.2°C). From a safety perspective, as long as you cook it long enough to pasteurize it, 135°F (57.2°C) is just as safe as 165°F (73.8°C).

Common Pork Temperatures
Medium Rare: 130°F to 139°F
  (54.4°C to 59.4°C)
Medium: 140°F to 145°F (60°C to 62.8°C)
Well Done: Above 145°F (62.8°C)

My favorite temperature for sous vide pork is 140°F (60°C), though I sometimes cook it lower when I want to put a solid sear on it.

Most people were raised on pork cooked above 155°F or 165°F (68.3°C or 73.8°C) and can't stand having any pink on the inside so 145°F (62.8°C) might work best for them. That's also the temperature I often do when I have guests that might be squeamish.

Traditional Braise-Like Texture

The most famous braise-like preparation is probably pulled pork, at least in America, but there are other dishes that are made including several braised cuts, BBQ, ribs, and other "low and slow" preparations. The cuts used for this are tough and generally high in fat and connective tissue, such as shoulder, butt, belly, shank, ribs, and many roasts.

As the food cooks at a higher temperature, the connective tissue breaks down, making the meat flaky and shreddable. The higher the temperature you use, and the longer you cook it, will cause the meat to break down more.

> **Common Braise-Like Temperatures**
> Most braise-like temperatures range from around 150°F up to 185°F (65.6°C up to 85°C). The temperatures I recommend starting with are:
>
> 156°F (68.8°C) for shreddable, but firm
> 165°F (73.9°C) for more fall apart
> 176°F (80.0°C) for really fall apart

When you are getting started, I recommend taking a favorite dish of yours such as pulled pork and trying it at all three temperatures. It'll give you a great idea of how the different temperatures affect the meat. Then you can tweak the temperature and the time it is cooked to meet your standards.

Sous Vide Pork Times

There are two main types of pork cuts: tender cuts and tough cuts. The cook times differ based on what type of cut you are using. You can follow the charts in the Cooking by Tenderness and Cooking by Thickness chapters for more specific suggestions.

Tender Cuts of Pork

For tender cuts you just need to cook them long enough to be pasteurized and then you can eat them. Common tender cuts are tenderloin, loin roast, most pork chops, and other cuts you would usually enjoy grilling or pan frying.

Tough Cuts of Pork

Longer cooking times are required to break down tough cuts of pork and make the meat tender. The time needed depends on the cut but usually is 18 hours to 2 days. Some favorite tough cuts are shoulder, ribs, and shank.

> **How Long to Pastuerize Pork**
> The time needed to pasteurize pork depends on the temperature, but at 140°F (60°C) it happens at the following rate:
>
> 0.5" (13mm) thick in 50 minutes
> 1" (25mm) thick in 80 minutes
> 1.5" (38mm) thick in 2 hours
> 2" (50mm) thick in 2.5 hours

How to Finish Pork

Finishing pork is usually done by drying it really well, salting it and then searing it. This gives it a much more appealing look and adds a lot of great flavor. You can sear it however you are most comfortable but I generally pan fry it or grill it.

I also often will use a torch, especially if it is an odd-shaped piece of meat. If I'm deep frying something else I'll often use the oil to deep fry the meat as well.

Whatever method you use, you will want to sear it very quickly to prevent it from overcooking any more than is necessary. You can read more about searing in the How to Sear Food chapter.

Some people also smoke their pork after it has been sous vided, especially for pulled pork and other barbecued meats. If you do this, it is usually best to chill it first for 10 to 20 minutes in an ice bath. Then when you are smoking it, make sure the temperature doesn't go above the temperature you sous vided it at.

Pork Chops with Broccolini and Roasted Peppers

Cooks: 140°F (60°C) for 2 to 3 hours • Serves: 4

Pork, much like chicken, is good at many different temperatures and people usually feel strongly about which one it should be cooked at. I prefer mine cooked at 140°F (60°C), leaving the middle a slight pink which is very moist and tender. However, people enjoy it anywhere between 135°F to 149°F (57.8°C to 65°C). So find the temperature you like for pork and stick with it.

The time just needs to be long enough to cook it through, and I usually pasteurize it just to be safe. You can refer to the Cooking by Thickness chapter for more information.

For the Pork Chop
- 4 pork chops, preferably thick cut
- 1 teaspoon garlic powder
- 1 teaspoon onion powder
- ½ teaspoon coriander
- 4 sprigs of thyme

For the Broccolini
- Olive oil
- 2 teaspoons diced garlic
- 2 bunches broccolini

For the Roasted Peppers
- 2 red bell peppers
- 2 yellow bell peppers
- Olive oil

To Assemble
- Olive oil
- Sea salt

For the Pork Chop

Preheat a water bath to 140°F (60°C).

Mix together the spices in a bowl. Lightly salt and pepper the pork chop then sprinkle with the spices. Place in a sous vide pouch with the thyme sprigs, then seal the bag and cook for 2 to 3 hours, until heated through or pasteurized.

For the Broccolini

Heat some olive oil in a pan over medium heat. Add the broccolini and garlic to the pan and cook until tender.

For the Roasted Peppers

Remove the stem and seeds of the peppers then cut into whole sides. Toss the peppers with olive oil then salt and pepper them. Cook under a broiler, or in a hot pan, until they have taken on color and become tender.

To Assemble

Remove the cooked pork chop from the bag and dry it off. Quickly sear the pork just until color develops.

Place the pork chop on a plate and surround with the bell peppers. Top with the broccolini then drizzle with olive oil and sprinkle with sea salt.

Italian Sausage with Onions and Peppers

Cooks: 140°F (60°C) for 2 to 3 hours • Serves: 4

Using sous vide to cook the sausage in this classic dish of sausage and peppers ensures a moist, perfectly cooked sausage. You can also eat this dish on a hoagie roll with melted provolone cheese on top. I prefer to finish the sausages on a grill, but you can use a hot pan or a torch if it's easier.

These sausages are also great if you are having pasta. Simply add the sausages, onions, and peppers to your favorite marinara sauce for a hearty meal.

For the Sausage
8 Italian sausage links

For the Onions and Peppers
2 onions
1 red pepper
1 orange pepper
1 poblano pepper

For the Sausage
Preheat the water bath to 140°F (60°C).

Place the sausage links in the sous vide pouches. Seal the pouches then place in the water bath and cook for 2 to 3 hours.

For the Onions and Peppers
Heat a grill to high heat.

Peel the onions and then cut into slices about ½" to ¾" thick, trying to keep the slices together. You can also thread the onion slices onto a shish-kabob skewer.

Cut the sides off of the peppers, leaving them whole. Salt and pepper the onions and peppers and then drizzle with the canola oil.

Add the onions and peppers and cook until they just begin to brown and are cooked through. Remove them from the heat. Once they have cooled enough to handle slice the peppers into ½" strips.

To Assemble
Remove the sausage from their pouches and pat them dry. Quickly sear them on two sides on the grill over high heat, about 1 or 2 minutes per side.

Plate the dish by spooning the peppers and onions onto a plate and topping with 2 sausage links per person.

Sous Vide St. Louis Ribs

Cooks: 156°F (68.8°C) for 8 to 12 hours • Serves: 4 to 8

There are many different suggestions for how long and what temperature to cook ribs. It can be confusing but the time and temperature combination you want to use depends on how you'd like your final ribs to turn out. The hotter the temperature, the faster they cook and the more they tenderize. The amount of time you cook them for determines how tender they end up. These time and temperature combinations work for most kinds of pork ribs, including St. Louis cut, baby back, back, and spare ribs.

If you prefer traditional-style ribs, then cooking them at 160°F to 167°F (71.1°C to 75°C) for 4 to 10 hours is what you want. These ribs are flaky and falling off the bone. Sous vide them for 4 hours for ribs with a lot of bite to them and for 10 hours for ribs barely hanging on the bone.

For tender ribs that are more pork chop-like you can cook them at 141°F to 149°F (60.6°C to 65°C) for 1 to 2 days. They do not have the texture of traditional ribs but retain a lot more of their moisture.

Cooking the ribs at a temperature in between those two extremes results in firmer, but still flaky, ribs. They don't fall off the bone but they are much closer to traditional ribs. I often cook mine at 156°F (68.8°C) for 8 to 12 hours.

For the Ribs

2 racks St. Louis ribs or baby back ribs
2 teaspoons smoked paprika
2 teaspoons celery salt
2 teaspoons garlic powder
1 teaspoon onion powder
1 teaspoon ancho chile powder
1 teaspoon ground coriander
1 teaspoon ground cumin
½ teaspoon mustard powder

To Assemble

BBQ Sauce

For the Ribs

Preheat a water bath to 156°F (68.8°C).

Trim any silver skin or connective tissue from the ribs if you want. Mix the spices together in a bowl. Salt and pepper the ribs then coat with the spice mixture, you may have some spice mixture leftover. Place the ribs in sous vide bags, cutting the racks in half if needed. Seal the bags and then cook for 8 to 12 hours.

To Assemble

Preheat a grill to high heat or the broiler in the oven.

Remove the ribs from the sous vide bags and pat dry. Brush the ribs with the BBQ sauce and sear them on the first side for a minute. Brush the BBQ sauce on the side facing up and turn the ribs. Repeat several times until it is coated with the glaze, cooking about 30 to 60 seconds per turn. Remove from the heat, brush once more with the BBQ sauce, and serve.

Pulled Pork with Chile Pepper BBQ Sauce

Cooks: 156°F (68.8°C) for 18 to 24 hours • Serves: 4 to 8

Pulled pork is usually made using the pork butt, sometimes called the pork shoulder or Boston Butt, and is cooked over low heat, often in a smoker, for several hours. Using sous vide takes longer but you don't have to manage a fire or look in on the meat. My favorite combination is probably 156°F (68.8°C) for around 18 to 24 hours, it's shreddable but not over-tender.

For a more traditional flavor, you can either pre- or post-smoke the pork shoulder, just make sure it is cold when you are smoking it. I like to serve it with traditional BBQ sides such as corn on the cob, coleslaw, or macaroni and cheese.

For the Pork Shoulder
2 to 3 pounds pork shoulder (900 to 1360 grams)
1 teaspoons sweet paprika
1 teaspoons garlic powder
1 teaspoon ancho chile powder
½ teaspoon cinnamon

For the Chile Pepper Sauce
4 to 7 dried chile peppers
Olive oil
⅓ cup tomato paste
¼ cup sherry vinegar
1 tablespoon Worcestershire sauce
¼ cup dark rum
2 tablespoons brown sugar
¾ cup water
1 tablespoon minced garlic
2 tablespoons honey
1 teaspoon paprika
1 teaspoon cumin
1 teaspoon coriander

To Assemble
BBQ Sides

For the Pork Shoulder
Preheat a water bath to 156°F (68.8°C).

If the pork shoulder is too large to fit in a bag, cut it into multiple pieces. Mix the spices together in a bowl then coat the pork with them. Place the pork in a sous vide bag then seal. Cook the pork for 18 to 24 hours.

For the Chile Pepper Sauce
Take the chile peppers and soak them in water for 30 minutes. Remove the stems and seeds.

Heat some olive oil in a pan over medium heat, add the tomato paste then cook until just starting to darken. Add the chile peppers and remaining ingredients and blend well. Bring the mixture to a simmer and let cook for at least 5 minutes for the flavors to meld, or up to 30 minutes if you want it thicker. If you prefer a thinner sauce, add more water until it is the desired consistency.

To Assemble
Remove the pork from the sous vide bag and shred it with a fork and tongs.

On a plate, make a pile of the pulled pork and top with the chile pepper BBQ sauce. Serve with your favorite BBQ sides.

Boar Tenderloin with Cherry Chutney

Cooks: 140°F (60°C) for 2 to 3 hours • Serves: 4

Boar behaves very similarly to pork but has a richer, sometimes nutty flavor. I like to prepare it just like pork, cooking it at 140°F (60°C) long enough to cook it through and pasteurize it.

Here I serve it with a sweet and spicy cherry chutney that complements the flavor of the meat really well. It also goes great with any sides you normally like to serve with pork, such as roasted vegetables, casserole, or a salad.

For the Boar Tenderloin
2 pounds boar tenderloin (900 grams)
1 teaspoon garlic powder
½ teaspoon coriander
½ teaspoon cumin
4 sprigs of rosemary

For the Cherry Chutney
Olive oil
¼ onion, diced
1 cup coarsely diced, pitted cherries, about 15
2 teaspoons minced ginger
1 tablespoon balsamic vinegar
2 tablespoons spiced rum
⅛ teaspoon chile powder, preferably chipotle
¼ teaspoon allspice
¼ teaspoon cinnamon

To Assemble
Fresh rosemary, minced

For the Boar Tenderloin
Preheat a water bath to 140°F (60°C).

Mix together the spices in a bowl. Lightly salt and pepper the boar tenderloin then sprinkle with the spices. Place in a sous vide pouch with the rosemary sprigs then seal the bag and cook for 2 to 3 hours, until heated through or pasteurized.

For the Cherry Chutney
Heat some olive oil in a pan over medium heat. Add the onion and cook until just starting to brown. Add the cherries and ginger and cook for 5 minutes. Add the remaining ingredients and cook until thickened to the desired consistency, adding water if needed. Taste and adjust seasonings as needed.

The cherry chutney can be held in the refrigerator for several days.

To Assemble
Remove the cooked boar tenderloin from the bag and dry it off. Quickly sear it just until color develops.

Place the boar tenderloin on a plate and top with the cherry chutney. Sprinkle with the rosemary then serve.

Chicken, Duck and Poultry

The next type of food I want to cover is chicken, turkey, and other poultry. I think sous vide transforms chicken and turkey breasts more than just about any other type of meat. They turn out so much more moist and tender than their traditional counterparts, in large part because you can cook them at a lower temperature.

In this chapter I'll show you how to get the most out of your sous vide chicken, turkey and other poultry.

What is Poultry?

Different places have different definitions of what poultry is. In this chapter I'm using it generically to refer to most birds such as chicken and turkey as well as duck, goose, quail, Cornish game hens, squab, and game birds such as pheasants.

Types of Poultry in Cooking

From a basic culinary perspective, there are two main types of poultry. I generally break them down by how their breast meat behaves and is cooked.

The first is birds with dense breast meat that is more like beef or other red meat. This would include duck and goose. In this chapter I'll refer this type of poultry as "medium rare poultry" because the breast meat is traditionally cooked medium rare.

The second type of poultry is those with lighter, less dense breast meat. This includes chicken, turkey, and quail. In this chapter I'll refer this type of poultry as "well done poultry" because the breast meat is traditionally cooked to higher temperatures.

Even though both types of breast meat are treated differently, most of the dark meat is cooked the same regardless of the type of poultry.

White and dark meat are generally cooked at different temperatures so it's often best to cook them separately.

Sous Vide Poultry Safety

A major concern with cooking chicken and poultry is ensuring that it is safe to eat. Traditionally, this meant cooking most chicken to at least 150°F to 165°F (65.5°C to 73.8°C). As we discussed in the chapter on sous vide safety guidelines, you can achieve the same safety levels through extended cooking times at lower temperatures. This allows you to enjoy much juicier poultry than you normally would.

Common Poultry Temperatures
Once heated, chicken and other poultry are pasteurized by cooking it at:

140°F (60.0°C) for 30 minutes
145°F (62.8°C) for 12 minutes
150°F (65.6°C) for 4 minutes

Warning: One concern is pathogens that might be present in wild or game birds. If you are eating wild animals, cooked with sous vide or traditionally, you should make yourself aware of the pathogens and what temperatures are needed to kill them.

Pre-Sous Vide Poultry Steps

When preparing sous vide poultry, you have a lot of options on how to approach it before you put it in the sous vide bag.

Many people prefer skinless and boneless poultry and it works just fine. That said, if it is cooked with the skin on and bone in, it does add additional flavor to the end result as well as making it easier to sear for a little longer.

Most poultry are simply seasoned with salt and pepper or a dry rub. Herbs or lemon are also good additions to the sous vide pouch.

Brining is not required with sous vide poultry and it generally doesn't have much of an effect on the final dish. However, for some preparations such as duck confit, the meat can first be cured in a dry rub to firm up the meat and introduce other flavors.

How to Sous Vide Breast Meat

As mentioned earlier, when cooking breast meat it's easiest to break it in to "Well Done" poultry like chicken, turkey, or quail and "Medium Rare" poultry like duck or goose.

Chicken, Turkey and Other "Well Done" Poultry

The two main considerations when cooking white meat from poultry usually cooked to a "well-done" temperature is safety and texture.

Sous Vide White Meat Safety

When cooking white meat you want to make sure you cook it long enough to pasteurize it. This can be done at any temperature above 130°F (54.4°C), though chicken is usually cooked above 136°F (57.7°C). The Pasteurization Times for Chicken in the Cooking by Tenderness chapter will give you specific times needed to pasteurize at several different temperatures.

Sous Vide White Meat Texture

So now that we've established that any temperature above 130°F (54.4°C) can be safe to eat, what temperature should you actually use? It really depends on your personal preference but my go-to temperature is 141°F (60.5°C).

White meat cooked at the lowest temperatures has a very unique texture. It's still very "raw" feeling and a little slimy. Some people really enjoy it but most people, especially those looking for a "normal" chicken breast, can't stand it.

Once you get around 137°F (58.3°C) the poultry starts to take on a "cooked" texture. The meat starts to firm up and dry out slightly, which in most people's opinion is a good thing. The higher the temperature used, the firmer and drier the meat becomes.

I've found 141°F (60.5°C) to be the sweet spot for me between maintaining a lot of moisture while still really tasting like a "normal" chicken breast. Most, if not all, of the pink color is gone and the breast is uniformly firm but tender.

For some people that's still too low of a temperature and they prefer their breast cooked at around 145°F (62.2°C). The chicken is less juicy but still more tender than most traditionally cooked breasts.

For a completely "normal" breast, you can cook it at 150°F to 160°F (65.5°C to 71.1°C) and it'll still be better than most regularly cooked chicken, though not nearly as moist or tender as the lower temperatures. Serious Eats looked at the amount of juice loss at different temperatures and discovered a chicken breast loses more than twice as much moisture at 150°F (65.5°C) than it does at 140°F (60°C).

Duck, Goose and Other "Medium Rare" Poultry

If you are cooking a bird that you normally would eat at a temperature besides well-done, you don't necessarily have to pasteurize it. If you would traditionally feel comfortable eating it at a lower temperature, then you just need to heat it through to the temperature you prefer.

Of course, with sous vide you can still pasteurize it at any temperature above 130°F (54.4°C) and that's usually what I do to be on the safe side.

For tender cuts of duck and goose like the breast, I cook them just enough to heat them through and pasteurize them at a medium-rare temperature. This normally takes 2 to 3 hours for temperatures from 129°F to 135°F (53.8°C to 57.2°C). I tend to use 131°F (55°C) when I cook it, though if you prefer medium then you'd probably like it cooked around 140°F (60°C).

How to Sous Vide Dark Meat

Most dark meat in poultry, such as chicken thighs and duck legs, is treated similarly to each other. You can either cook them to be tender, like a typical seared or roasted thigh or you can cook them to be shreddable, like confit duck legs.

The temperature used to create tender dark meat is usually between 141°F up to 156°F (60.6°C up to 68.9°C). I personally like 148°F (64.4°C) the best because I think it delivers the best mix of texture and juiciness. Most dark meat doesn't need to be tenderized much, if at all, so the time range is typically 2 to 5 hours to fully pasteurize them.

For shreddable dark meat, the range goes much higher but is often between 145°F to 170°F (62.7°C to 76.7°C). I usually split the difference and use 165°F (73.9°C). They are cooked longer as well to allow for more breakdown, usually for 8 to 12 hours, or even longer at the lower end of the temperature range.

How to Finish Poultry

Finishing poultry is usually done by drying it really well, salting it and then searing it. This gives it a much more appealing look and adds a lot of great flavor.

You can sear it however you are most comfortable but I generally pan fry it or grill it. Using a torch can also be effective for some cuts of poultry but I generally stick to pan frying.

For certain preparations, such as fried chicken or turkey piccata, you can also coat the sous vided meat before pan frying or deep frying it.

Whatever method you use, you will want to sear it very quickly to prevent it from overcooking any more than is necessary. You can read more in the How to Sear Food chapter.

For preparations when the chicken will not be visible, I'll sometimes just skip the sear, keeping the chicken as tender as possible.

Spring Salad with Chicken Breast

Cooks: 141°F (60.5°C) for 2 to 4 hours • Serves: 4

This recipe really helps to show how much a perfectly cooked chicken breast can transform a simple salad. I'll often use a spice rub on my chicken breasts to add flavor. This recipe calls for a vindaloo seasoning but you can use any of your favorite spice rubs.

I almost always cook my chicken breasts at 141°F (60.5°C) until pasteurized, but you can go up or down in temperature as you see fit.

I like to finish the chicken on the grill, but you can sear it anyway you want...sometimes I'm just too hungry and eat it without a sear!

For the Sous Vide Chicken
4 chicken breasts
3 tablespoons vindaloo seasoning or other spice mixture

For the Vinaigrette
3 tablespoons white wine vinegar
1 shallot, minced
4 to 6 tablespoons olive oil

To Assemble
4 plates of mixed lettuce
1 yellow pepper, cut into slices
6 to 8 radishes, thinly sliced
½ cup blueberries
¼ cup roasted seeds or sunflower seeds

For the Sous Vide Chicken

Preheat the water bath to 141°F (60.5°C).

Salt and pepper the chicken and sprinkle with about 1 tablespoon of the spice mixture. Add to the sous vide pouches, seal, and place in the water bath. Cook the chicken for 2 to 4 hours.

For the Vinaigrette

To make the vinaigrette combine the vinegar and shallot in a bowl and let sit for 5 minutes. Slowly whisk in the olive oil until emulsified. Salt and pepper to taste.

To Assemble

Preheat a grill to high heat.

Take the sous vide chicken out of the pouches and pat dry. Sear the chicken on a very hot grill for 45 to 60 seconds per side. Remove from the heat.

To serve, place the greens in individual bowls or on plates. Top with the bell pepper, radishes, and blue berries. Add the chicken and spoon the vinaigrette on top. Add the roasted seeds and serve.

Honey-Sriracha Glazed Chicken Legs

Cooks: 148°F (64.4°C) for 2 to 5 hours • Serves: 4

This recipe shows a great way to add flavor to chicken post-sous vide by using a sweet and spicy honey-sriracha glaze. You can vary the amount of sriracha and honey in your glaze to make it as hot or as sweet as you like.

This recipe will work well with most types of poultry legs and thighs. I've found that searing chicken legs works best on a grill or under a hot broiler because of their odd shape.

For the Chicken Legs

2 pounds chicken legs (900 grams)

5-spice powder

For the Honey-Sriracha Glaze

3 tablespoons honey

2 tablespoons sriracha sauce or other chile sauce

1 tablespoon rice wine vinegar

1 tablespoon soy sauce

For the Squash

Olive oil

2 zucchini, cut into long strips

2 yellow squash, cut into long strips

To Assemble

Fresh basil

Sesame seeds, preferably black and white

Sesame oil

For the Chicken Legs

Preheat a water bath to 148°F (64.4°C).

Lightly salt and pepper the chicken legs then sprinkle with the 5-spice powder. Place in a sous vide pouch then seal the bag and cook for 2 to 5 hours.

For the Honey-Sriracha Glaze

Mix together all the ingredients. This can be done ahead of time and stored in a sealed container in the refrigerator for a few days.

For the Squash

Heat some olive oil over medium-high heat. Add the squash sticks and cook until tender, about 5 to 10 minutes, turning occasionally.

To Assemble

Remove the cooked chicken legs from the bag and dry them off. Brush the glaze on them and quickly sear until the glaze begins to bubble, turning regularly. Repeat a few times to get a thick glaze on the legs.

Place the squash on a plate and top with some chicken legs. Sprinkle with the basil, sesame seeds and sesame oil.

Turkey Breast with Roasted Apples and Tomatoes

Cooks: 140°F (60°C) for 4 to 8 hours • Serves: 4

If you are looking for super-moist, tender turkey breast then it's really hard to beat sous vide turkey. There's a definite art to properly roasting an entire turkey and getting every part to turn out perfectly cooked, and it's something that's always hit or miss for me. Once I switched to sous vide turkey breast, I make awesome turkey every time.

If you really love crisp skin, you can remove it from the breast and crisp it up in the oven around serving time. There are several ways to do it but treating it like bacon and using a skillet on medium-heat with a little oil works well. You can also place it on parchment paper on a baking sheet with raised edges, add another layer of parchment paper and then another baking sheet on top and bake it in an oven set to 375°F to 400°F until it's nice and brown, usually for 40 minutes.

You have several options for the turkey breast meat itself. My favorite is to cook it at 140°F (60°C) for 4 to 8 hours which I think results in the best combination of "moist but cooked" so it's what I often go with.

For the Turkey Breast
2 turkey breasts, ideally bones attached
1 lemon
10 sage leaves

For the Roasted Apples
3 sweet apples such as gala or honey crisp
2 tablespoons brown sugar
⅛ teaspoon cinnamon
⅛ teaspoon cloves

To Assemble
Cherry tomatoes

For the Sous Vide Turkey Breast
Preheat a water bath to 140°F (60°C).

Salt the turkey breasts and add to a sous vide bag. Remove the zest from the lemon, using a vegetable peeler or zester and place in the bag on the turkey breasts. Add the sage leaves to the bag then seal it.

Cook the turkey breasts for 4 to 8 hours, or at a minimum, until they are pasteurized.

For the Roasted Apples
Preheat an oven to 400°F (204°C).

Remove the stem and seeds from the apples then cut into eights. Toss the apples with the sugar, cinnamon and cloves. Take a baking sheet with a rim and spread the apples out in a single layer. Bake until tender, about 30 to 40 minutes, flipping the apples after 20 minutes.

To Assemble
Once cooked, remove the cooked turkey breasts from the sous vide bag and pat dry. Lightly salt the outside then quickly sear them until just browned. You can serve the turkey breasts whole or cut them into slices.

Spoon the apples on a plate and set the turkey breasts around them with the cherry tomatoes, then serve.

Duck Breast with Blackberry Port Sauce

Cooks: 131°F (55°C) for 2 to 3 hours • Serves: 4

Here is a simple to make duck recipe that always turns out great. You can use this general recipe for most other "medium-rare" poultry as well. I cook it just long enough to heat it through and pasteurize it, usually 2 to 3 hours. My temperature of choice is 131°F (55°C), but you can raise or lower it to your preference.

Duck is one of my favorite meats to eat. I love the combination of tender meat with rich, creamy fat. In this recipe I pair it with some grilled asparagus and a blackberry-port sauce. I use a few unusual garnishes with this dish since I was growing them in my garden but feel free to use the more common versions, or any garnish of your choosing.

When searing, you can let the duck go a little bit longer on the fat side to get more rendered out. You can even chill the duck first for 5 to 10 minutes in an ice bath so they can get a better sear.

For the Duck Breast
3 duck breasts
2 teaspoons ground coriander
1 teaspoon smoked paprika
½ teaspoon ground cumin

For the Blackberry-Port Sauce
1 pint blackberries
1 cup port

For the Grilled Asparagus
1-2 bunches thin asparagus
Canola oil
¼ lemon

To Assemble
Fresh lemon thyme, or thyme leaves
Fresh Greek basil, or Italian basil leaves
Ripe blackberries
Nasturtium flower, optional
Olive oil
Flaky sea salt

For the Duck Breast
Preheat a water bath to 131°F (55°C).

Mix together the spices in a bowl. Salt and pepper the duck breast then coat it with the spices. Place the duck breast in a sous vide bag then seal. Cook the duck for 2 to 3 hours.

For the Blackberry-Port Sauce
Combine the blackberries and port then puree well with a standing or immersion blender. Strain the seeds out of the puree using a coarse strainer. Put puree in a pot or pan and bring to a simmer, then let reduce to the desired thickness.

The blackberry-port sauce can be made several hours ahead of time.

For the Grilled Asparagus
Heat a grill to high heat.

Toss the asparagus with the canola oil, salt, and pepper. Place on the grill and cook, turning once or twice, until softened. Remove from the heat. Squeeze the lemon over the asparagus.

To Assemble
Remove the cooked duck from the sous vide bag and pat dry. Lightly salt the outside of the duck breast then quickly sear it until the outside has browned and the fat has begun to render. Cut the duck into slices.

Place a spoonful or two of the blackberry-port sauce on a plate or bowl. Lay a few slices of the sous vide duck breast on top with some asparagus spears. Sprinkle some lemon thyme leaves and Greek basil over the top. Add a few blackberries and nasturtium flowers around the sides. Drizzle with olive oil and sprinkle with sea salt then serve.

Shredded Duck Legs with Sesame Noodles

Cooks: 167°F (75°C) for 16 to 24 hours • Serves: 4

My wife always orders cold sesame noodles from our local Chinese restaurant so I decided to try and make my own. I found this version to be the most flavorful and the one that I could easily find all the ingredients for at my local supermarket. It's topped with shredded duck legs because they can hold up to the strong flavors of the noodles. You can either eat this dish hot or cold, it's great either way. You can add more or less chile-garlic paste depending on how spicy you want it.

There are a few options when you want to shred duck legs. Many people recommend 167°F (75°C) for at least 8 hours and up to 24 hours. This time and temperature combination also works well for duck confit. Cooking them at 144°F (62.2°C) for 18 to 24 hours is also highly recommended for a less fall-apart texture.

Duck legs can also be lightly cured first to add flavor, which is something I do for this recipe. Just spice the duck legs, cover them with salt and sugar, then let them sit for up to 12 hours.

For the Duck Legs

- 4 duck legs, about 3 pounds (1360 grams)
- 4 cups salt
- ½ cup sugar
- 3 tablespoons ground coriander
- 4 garlic cloves, minced
- 2 tablespoons orange zest
- 1 tablespoon ground cloves
- 1 teaspoon black pepper, coarsely ground
- 1 bay leaf, crushed

For the Sesame Noodles

- 12 ounces Chinese egg noodles or soba noodles, (340 grams)
- 3 tablespoons sesame oil, preferably dark
- 3 tablespoons soy sauce
- 2 tablespoons rice wine vinegar
- 2 tablespoons sesame paste or tahini
- 2 tablespoons peanut butter, preferably smooth
- 2 tablespoons brown sugar
- 1 tablespoon chile-garlic paste, such as sambal
- 2 garlic cloves, minced
- 2 scallions, thinly sliced
- Sesame seeds
- 1 1" (25mm) piece of ginger, peeled and minced

To Assemble

- 1 cucumber, julienned
- 1 carrot, peeled and julienned or grated
- 1 cup bean sprouts
- Peanuts, roughly chopped
- Fresh cilantro, chopped
- Sesame seeds, preferably toasted

For the Duck Legs

Mix together the salt and sugar in a bowl. In a separate bowl mix together the remaining spices then coat the duck legs with them. Place the duck legs in a plastic bag or non-reactive container and pack the salt and sugar cure evenly around them. Refrigerate for 8 to 12 hours.

Preheat a water bath to 167°F (75°C).

Wash the cure off of the duck legs then place in a sous vide bag and seal. Cook the duck for 16 to 24 hours.

Once cooked, remove the duck from the sous vide bag and pat dry. Sear the duck legs in a hot pan until crispy. Remove the meat from the bones and shred.

For the Sesame Noodles

Bring a pot of water to a boil and then add the noodles. Cook until tender but still slightly firm. Drain the noodles.

Blend together the sesame oil, soy sauce, rice wine vinegar, sesame paste, peanut butter, and brown sugar. Stir in the chile-garlic paste, garlic, scallions, sesame seeds, and ginger. Toss the noodles with the sauce. If serving cold you can let them cool and then refrigerate them at this point.

To Assemble

Place a pile of noodles on a plate or in a bowl. Top with the cucumber, carrots, and sprouts. Add the peanuts then the shredded duck. Sprinkle with the cilantro and sesame seeds, then serve.

Fish and Shellfish

In this chapter we are going to tackle sous vide fish. Fish is one of the hardest items to recommend times and temperatures for due to the wide variety of preferences people have, ranging from sushi (or sushi-like) to flaky and fully cooked, and the wide variety of fish available.

Fish are also a lot more sensitive than many items you sous vide and sometimes small temperature variations can result in large swings in texture. There is also such a wide variety of fish that it is hard to make blanket statements that will apply to all of them.

I'll try to give you my preferences for fish and explain what other people like and why they like it. Hopefully then you will have the information you need to successfully cook sous vide fish to your own tastes.

Sous Vide Fish Safety

Unless you are heating your fish above 130°F (54.4°C) for an extended time, only use fish that you would feel safe eating raw and you are not serving it to immunodeficient people.

This is true not only of sous vided fish, but also of fish cooked in a traditional manner. Most fish is never cooked to safe levels regardless of how it is cooked so you need to make sure it's high quality.

Buying your fish through a reputable fish monger will help ensure that it is fresh and of adequate quality that you should have no problems eating it.

Pre-Sous Vide Fish Preparation

There are a few things you can do before cooking the fish to make it both more flavorful and more appealing when cooking with sous vide.

Brining Sous Vide Fish
The top suggestion is to brine your fish before you cook it. The brine will help firm up the fish, especially when it is cooked at low temperatures, and will also pull out the albumin, resulting in a cleaner finished dish.

The brine can either take the form of a wet brine or a dry brine.

Wet Brine
A wet brine is usually a 5% salt to water ratio, and is applied for 5 to 15 minutes, depending on the fish. Make sure the brine is cool when the fish is added.

A 5% brine can be made by combining about 4 cups of water with ¼ cup kosher salt, heating it until the salt dissolves, then chilling it. Some brines also have sugar or spices added.

Dry Brine

A dry brine is easy to use, just salt the fish and refrigerate it for at least 30 minutes before cooking it. Dry brines typically result in a less watered down flavor and are faster to apply since you do not have to heat and cool water.

Portion the Fish

I recommend portioning out the fish before you sous vide it as well. Most fish becomes very delicate once it comes out of the sous vide bath and can tend to fall apart. Cutting it into portions first makes it much easier to handle.

Add Some Fat

If you are cooking more than one piece of fish in the same bag, it is usually best to add some olive oil or butter as well. This will help prevent the pieces from sticking together.

Sealing Sous Vide Fish

The flesh of fish is generally soft so be careful when vacuum sealing it. A strong vacuum can crush the flesh of the fish and change the texture. I often just use Ziploc bags when cooking fish because there is no added pressure to the fish itself, the cook times are short and the temperatures used are lower.

Sous Vide Fish Temperatures

There is a wide range of doneness you can shoot for when cooking fish sous vide. A lot of this will depend on your personal preferences and the type of fish you are eating.

The lowest temperature most people use is 104°F (40°C). This just slightly heats the fish through, releasing some flavor but doesn't really change the texture. There are similar results at temperatures up to about 110°F (43.3°C). This fish is basically sushi-like.

From 110°F to 120°F (43.3°C to 48.9°C) the fish generally begins to have more pronounced texture changes, becoming slightly more flaky and firm, while still retaining a lot of moisture.

Above 120°F (48.9°C) the fish starts to become more and more flaky and starts to dry out. The top temperature I usually cook any fish at is 132°F (55.5°C), though some people like it up to 140°F (60°C).

> **Warning:** Only temperatures above 130°F (54.4°C) will pasteurize the fish, and only when held for several hours, something that is usually not done with fish. I highly recommend only using fish you would feel comfortable eating raw, and not serving it to any immunodeficient people.

Different types of fish are best at different temperatures, so it's usually best to look at a recipe for a specific fish, or a similar type of fish, when you are trying to determine what temperature is right for the preparation you are after. I've provided some recipes here and a more detailed look at specific fish in the Cooking by Tenderness chapter.

Sous Vide Fish Times

Almost all fish only needs to be heated through and not tenderized, this results in much shorter cooking times than most types of food.

> **Common Fish Times**
> The length of time needed to heat it through depends on the thickness:
>
> 0.5" (13mm) thick in 14 minutes
> 1" (25mm) thick in 35 minutes
> 1.5" (38mm) thick in 1 hour 25 minutes
> 2" (50mm) thick in 2 hours

While those times generally work, many people don't cook their fish more than an hour because it can start to degrade in the water bath. Using a shorter time on a thicker piece of fish means the middle will be cooler, but this generally isn't a bad thing.

You can follow the charts for fish cooking times in the Cooking by Thickness chapter for the specific amount of time based on the thickness of your fish.

How to Finish Fish

Depending on your preparation, you can decide to sear the fish or skip the searing step. For lower temperature cooks, the sear is often not needed. This is also true for "poached" preparations where you want to keep the flavor and texture delicate.

For some preparations, you will want to dry off the fish really well then quickly sear it. Fish can overcook quickly, so you shouldn't go more than 30 to 60 seconds per side.

I will also often just sear one side of the fish, resulting in a better crust and presentation, while reducing the risk of over cooking it. This also helps prevent the fish from falling apart when you try to flip it multiple times.

You can also chill the fish briefly in an ice bath to give you more leeway on the searing time.

Most fish is eaten right after you cook it, but some fish is best chilled afterwards. This is usually done by leaving it in the sous vide pouch and dunking it in ice water. It can then be refrigerated until it is time to serve it. This will help the fish stay safe to eat and help prevent it from breaking apart.

Ask Jason: What is "Sushi Quality" Fish

"Your recipe calls for "Sushi Quality" fish, what the heck is that? I'm sous viding the fish, not eating it raw so what does sushi have to do with it? Thanks!"—Suzanne

Many sous vide fish recipes specify using "high quality" or "sushi quality" fish. While it's always good to use higher quality ingredients, it is important from a safety standpoint for lower-temperature fish recipes (anything cooked below 130°F to 140°F (54.4°C to 60.0°C).

Without going into too many details, many different pathogens can be present in different fish, based on the type of fish, how and where it was caught, and how and where it was stored. Certain fish are designed to be eaten raw as sushi or sashimi, or cooked to only low temperatures, while other fish are assumed they will be cooked to higher temperatures.

When planning to cook fish to a low temperature, whether this is using sous vide or traditional methods, you want to pick fish that you would feel safe eating raw. The low temperatures used will not kill all the pathogens that might be present, so it's important to use fish that are already safe to eat.

This is similar to picking beef to use for hamburgers or tartare. The inside of hamburgers usually doesn't become fully cooked unless you are cooking them to well-done so you need to use higher quality, "cleaner" beef than if you were just grilling or searing it.

This safety issue regarding low-temperature fish has really become more widespread through the use of sous vide, but it has always been present whenever fish has been cooked to rare or medium rare. Many people were not aware of the potential hazards of not fully cooking their fish, especially if the fish isn't high quality.

Whenever you are cooking fish to a lower internal temperature, just make sure you are using high quality fish and you should be fine!

Shrimp and Quinoa Bowl

Cooks: 130°F (54.4°C) for 15 to 35 minutes • Serves: 4

Shrimp cooked sous vide is always plump and juicy, with none of the rubberiness you can find in the pan fried version. Here I combine it with a filling quinoa salad filled with spinach, black beans and roasted red peppers, all topped off with tangy feta cheese!

There are a lot of temperatures you can use to cook shrimp but for "normal" shrimp I prefer 130°F (54.4°C). Some people like it cooked lower, down to 122°F (50°C) and others like it a little tougher at 140°F (60°C). Experiment with the different temperatures and see what works best for you!

For the Shrimp
1 pound shrimp, peeled and cleaned (450 grams)
½ teaspoon sweet paprika
½ teaspoon garlic powder

For the Vinaigrette
3 tablespoons white wine vinegar
2 tablespoons orange juice
1 tablespoon honey
1 shallot, diced
5 tablespoons olive oil

To Assemble
2 cups cooked quinoa
1 cup baby spinach leaves
½ cup cooked corn kernels
½ cup cooked black beans
¼ cup diced roasted red peppers
¼ red onion, diced
½ cucumber, diced
¼ cup crumbled feta cheese

For the Shrimp
Preheat a water bath to 130°F (54.4°C).

Place the shrimp in a sous vide bag in a single layer. Seal the bag then cook for 15 to 35 minutes, until heated through.

For the Vinaigrette
Whisk together the vinegar, orange juice, and honey. Stir in the shallot and let sit for 10 minutes. Slowly whisk in the olive oil until fully emulsified. Salt and pepper to taste.

To Assemble
Combine all the ingredients in a bowl then divvy up into individual bowls. Remove the shrimp from the bag and add to the bowls. Drizzle the vinaigrette over the top and serve.

Swordfish in Dashi with Snow Peas

Cooks: 130°F (54.4°C) for 30 to 45 minutes • Serves: 4

This dish is my take on an amazing course I had at Serpico in Philadelphia. This version combines tender swordfish with a light dashi garnished with snow peas, radishes, and cucumbers.

I cook the swordfish at 130°F (54.4°C) so it is on the more traditional side of the sous vide fish spectrum with a light and flaky texture, though you can use any of the fish temperatures you prefer. It just needs to be cooked long enough to heat through.

The dashi should be chilled so plan ahead for the time that takes. The fish will cool down once it's in the dashi, resulting in a fun cool and warm sensation as you eat it with the cold dashi.

For the Dashi
3 4" (100mm) pieces of kelp or kombu
2 quarts water
2 cups bonito flakes or katsuobushi

For the Swordfish
1 to 2 pounds swordfish steaks (450 to 900 grams)
1 lemon
1 tablespoon butter

To Assemble
Snow peas, julienned
Pink radish, thinly sliced
Cucumber, diced
Mint leaves, minced
Mirin
Sesame oil
Lemon wedges

For the Dashi
Remove some of the powdery coating from the kombu by gently wiping it with a damp cloth or paper towel. Add the kombu to a pot and cover with the water. Soak for 45 minutes.

Slowly heat the water to 160°F (71.1°C) over medium heat, this should take about 10 minutes. Remove the kombu from the pot and discard.

Turn the heat up to high and bring to a boil. Add the bonito flakes and remove from the heat. Let steep for 5 minutes. Strain the liquid to remove the bonito and any floating particles. Let the dashi cool and then place in the refrigerator to fully chill.

The dashi can be stored in the refrigerator for a week.

For the Swordfish
Preheat a water bath to 130°F (54.4°C).

Clean the swordfish and cut into portions if needed. Liberally salt and pepper the swordfish then zest the lemon over the top. Place the swordfish in a sous vide bag with the butter then seal. Let the swordfish sit for 30 minutes for the dry brine to take effect.

Cook the swordfish for 30 to 45 minutes, until heated through.

To Assemble
Remove the fish from the bag and pat dry. Briefly sear the swordfish on one side.

Place the fish in the middle of a shallow bowl with the seared side up. Set some snow peas, radish slices and cucumber around the fish. Sprinkle some mint leaves on top of the fish. Pour the dashi around the fish. Drizzle some mirin and sesame oil in the dashi, squeeze a lemon wedge over the fish then serve.

Sea Bass with Microgreens and Mustard Oil

Cooks: 120°F (48.8°C) for 25 to 40 minutes • Serves: 4

Sea bass is a light and flavorful fish and I try not to overpower its taste when I serve it. The recipe pairs it with a pungent mustard oil that really shines with a basil, radish, and tomato salad with microgreens. If you can't find microgreens, any spring lettuce mix can act as a substitute.

The sea bass is cooked at 120°F (48.8°C) until just heated through, which generally takes 25 to 40 minutes. It comes out very tender and soft, almost like slightly cooked sashimi. You can go higher or lower with the temperature as you see fit though.

The mustard oil is best when made ahead of time, so be sure to start it a day or two before you want to eat.

For the Mustard Oil

2 tablespoons yellow mustard seeds

2 tablespoons brown mustard seeds

2 cups olive oil

For the Sea Bass

1 to 2 pounds sea bass, cut into portions and skin removed (450 to 900 grams)

1 teaspoon garlic powder

1 tablespoon butter

To Assemble

Pink radish, thinly sliced

Cherry tomatoes, halved

Microgreens

Basil leaves

Lemon, quartered

For the Mustard Oil

Combine the mustard seeds and olive oil in a pot and set over low heat. Bring to a sizzle then remove from the heat and let cool to room temperature. Pour in a non-reactive container, cover and refrigerate overnight. Strain the oil to remove the seeds. The oil will keep in the refrigerator for several days.

For the Sea Bass

Preheat a water bath to 120°F (48.8°C).

Clean the sea bass and cut into portions if needed. Liberally salt and pepper the sea bass then sprinkle with the garlic powder. Place the fish in a sous vide bag with the butter then seal. Let the sea bass sit for 30 minutes for the dry brine to take effect.

Cook the fish until heated through, about 25 to 40 minutes.

To Assemble

Remove the fish from the bag and pat dry. Briefly sear the fish if desired.

Place the sea bass in the middle of a plate. Set some radish slices and tomato halves around the fish. Drizzle some of the mustard oil around the fish. Add some microgreens and basil to the top of the fish. Squeeze the lemon over the top and serve.

Sesame Crusted Tuna with Avocado Salad

Cooks: 110°F (43.3°C) for 20 to 60 minutes • Serves: 4

I love a nicely seared piece of tuna that is rare on the inside, but cooking it at a very low temperature with sous vide ensures that it is evenly cooked throughout. It also softens the fish slightly, making it even more delicious. You aren't trying to really cook the tuna so stick to a low temperature, I usually do 110°F (43.3°C) until it is just heated through.

For the Tuna
2 large tuna steaks
¼ cup olive oil

For the Avocado Salad
3 tablespoons peanut oil
1 tablespoon sesame oil
2 tablespoons lime juice
1 tablespoon rice vinegar
2 tablespoons soy sauce
1 tablespoon fish sauce
2 tablespoons grated fresh ginger
1 shallot, minced
½ serrano chile, minced
1 avocado, diced
1 cucumber, cut into half moons
2 carrots, peeled and julienned
¼ cup peanuts, chopped
1 scallion, thinly sliced

To Assemble
Canola oil
¼ cup black sesame seeds
¼ cup white sesame seeds

For the Tuna
Preheat a water bath to 110°F (43.3°C).

Salt and pepper the tuna then place in a sous vide bag. Add the olive oil then seal. Cook until heated through, 20 to 60 minutes.

For the Avocado Salad
Whisk together the peanut oil, sesame oil, lime juice, vinegar, soy sauce and fish sauce. Whisk in the ginger, shallot, and serrano chile. Toss the remaining ingredients with the dressing.

To Assemble
Heat the canola oil in a pan over medium to medium-high heat.

Combine the sesame seeds in a bowl. Remove the tuna from the bag, pat dry, and coat with the sesame seeds. Sear on the top and bottom until the sesame seeds become fragrant and begin to toast. Remove from the heat and slice into ½" strips (13mm).

Place several slices of the tuna on a plate. Add the avocado salad to the side then serve.

Lobster Tail with Tomato and Corn Salad

Cooks: 131°F (55°C) for 20 to 40 minutes • Serves: 4

Lobster cooked sous vide is tender and succulent, and this recipe showcases it with a simple tomato and corn salad. I prefer my lobster cooked at 131°F (55°C), but 140°F (60°C) will give you a more traditional texture. For a much softer texture you can drop the temperature lower.

To remove the lobster from the shell, you can either cut the shell off with kitchen shears, or boil the lobster for 1 to 2 minutes and chill it in an ice bath.

For the Lobster Tails
4 lobster tails, shell removed
4 tablespoons butter
8 basil leaves

For the Tomato and Corn Salad
2 cups diced fresh tomatoes
1 cup cooked corn kernels
1 avocado, diced
8 basil leaves
1 tablespoons lemon juice
2 tablespoons olive oil

To Assemble
1 lemon, cut into eighths
Sea salt

For the Lobster Tails
Preheat a water bath to 131°F (55°C).

Place all the ingredients in a sous vide bag then seal. Cook until heated through, 20 to 40 minutes.

For the Tomato and Corn Salad
Combine all the ingredients in a bowl and toss well to combine. Salt and pepper to taste.

To Assemble
Place a large spoonful of the tomato and corn sald onto a plate. Remove the lobster from the sous vide pouches and place one on top of the tomato salad. Spoon some of the butter out of the sous vide bag on to the lobster. Squeeze some lemon over the top, sprinkle with the sea salt and then serve.

Vegetables and Fruits

When it comes to using sous vide to cook food, there's one aspect that is often overlooked: sous vide vegetables and fruits. There's a lot of talk about steak, chicken and other meat but many people ignore the vegetables at first. While I do think sous vide has the biggest benefits with meat, it does make some dang tasty vegetables that some people swear by!

Pre-Sous Vide Vegetable Preparation

Preparing fruits and vegetables for sous vide follows a very similar process to preparing them for traditional cooking.

You will generally want to first wash and clean the vegetables. And in many cases peel or remove the skin from them.

It also helps if you portion out the vegetables ahead of time and cut them into relatively uniform sizes. This will help ensure they will all cook evenly.

Due to the high temperatures involved in cooking vegetables, I also recommend that you start pre-heating your water bath ahead of time since it can take a while.

Sealing Fruits and Vegetables

Fruits and vegetables are usually sealed very similarly to other things you are sous viding. In most cases they are also firm and can take a vacuum without being crushed.

When bagging your fruits and vegetables, make sure they are in a single layer in the bag to ensure even cooking.

They also tend to release more gas than meat does so you will need to check occasionally to make sure your bags are not floating. You may need to use a sous vide rack or weight the bags down to keep them underwater. Magnets work great for this as well. You can review the section on preventing floating bags in the How to Seal Food chapter.

Vegetable Times and Temperatures

Similar to meat, vegetables are affected differently by different temperatures, but their range is generally much smaller.

Most vegetables are held together with pectin and pectin only begins to break down above 180°F to 183°F (82.2°C to 83.9°C). This means almost all vegetables are cooked at least at 183°F (83.9°C). Hotter temperatures will cook the vegetables more quickly, but basically will have the same texture at the end.

The normal cook time for sous vide fruits and vegetables is generally between 25 and 90 minutes, with the tougher vegetables taking longer. The longer they cook, the more tender they will get.

There is a lot of variety in fruits and vegetables, so be aware that all cooking times will be estimates. For example, a late-season, ripe Bosc pear will cook much faster than an early-season, slightly under ripe one, not to mention a Bartlett Pear.

Asparagus with Dijon Mustard Vinaigrette

Cooks: 183°F (83.9°C) for 10 to 30 minutes • Serves: 4 as a side

Asparagus cooked sous vide is similar to blanched asparagus but ends up with a stronger flavor and slightly firmer texture. Because asparagus is so tender to start with you only need a short cooking time, usually 10 to 30 minutes, depending on the thickness of the asparagus. For thicker asparagus it can be helpful to peel off the tougher outer layer and they might need a little longer in the water bath.

This recipe works good with other tender vegetables as well, such as green beans and pea pods.

Asparagus and Dijon mustard pair really well so I make a simple Dijon vinaigrette to dress the finished asparagus with. It adds tangy base flavors while not overpowering the asparagus itself.

For the Asparagus
2 bunches asparagus

For the Dijon Vinaigrette
1 tablespoon white wine vinegar
1 tablespoon lemon juice
1 ½ tablespoons Dijon mustard
¼ cup olive oil
2 tablespoons chopped tarragon

To Assemble
Fresh tarragon, chopped

For the Asparagus
Preheat the water bath to 183°F (83.9°C).

Place the asparagus in a sous vide bag, trying to keep the thickness of the bag less than 1" (25mm) for even cooking. Salt and pepper the asparagus then seal the bag. Place in the water bath and cook for 10 to 30 minutes.

Once the asparagus is tender remove it from the bag.

For the Dijon Vinaigrette
Combine all the ingredients and whisk or blend together. The vinaigrette can be made several hours ahead of time and re-whisked just before serving.

To Assemble
Place the asparagus on a plate and drizzle the Dijon mustard vinaigrette over the top. Sprinkle the tarragon on top and serve.

Miso Glazed Turnips

Cooks: 183°F (83.9°C) for 45 to 60 minutes • Serves: 4 as a side

Using sous vide to glaze turnips is a simple process that results in a great side dish, especially when combined with umami-rich miso. You can also briefly cook turnips and their juices in a pan after sous viding them to reduce the sauce for a richer dish. This recipe also works well for other root vegetables such as carrots, radishes, and parsnips.

For the Turnips

2 to 4 turnips, peeled and cut into 1" wedges
1 tablespoon miso
1 tablespoon butter or olive oil
1 teaspoon sweet paprika

To Assemble

Honey
1 lemon
2 scallions, sliced

For the Turnips

Preheat the water bath to 183°F (83.9°C).

Combine all ingredients in a bowl and toss to mix well. Pour into a sous vide bag, trying to keep the thickness of the bag less than 1" (25mm) for even cooking, and seal. Place in the water bath and cook for 45 to 60 minutes.

Once the turnips are tender remove them from the water bath.

To Assemble

Pour the turnips and their juices into a pan and heat over medium-high heat until the juices have thickened. Drizzle with the honey and squeeze some lemon juice, about ¼ of a lemon, over the top. Cook until the sauce has thickened. Remove from the heat and serve with some lemon zest and scallions on top.

Curried Butternut Squash Soup

Cooks: 183°F (83.9°C) for 1 to 4 hours • Serves: 4

Making pureed soups is very easy to do with sous vide. Cooking the vegetables for between one and four hours allows them to break down fully, making it easy to simply add some liquid and puree them into a soup.

This version is a curried butternut squash but it works well with most winter squashes. With slight variations it also works with many root vegetables. You can add more or less curry paste, depending on how spicy you want it.

For the Butternut Squash
- 1 medium butternut squash, about 2 pounds (900 grams)
- 3 garlic cloves, peeled and coarsely chopped
- 1 tablespoon freshly grated ginger
- 2 teaspoons red curry paste
- 1 tablespoon butter or olive oil
- Juice from ½ of a lime
- ½ cup vegetable broth or chicken stock
- ¼ cup coconut milk

To Assemble
- 2 shallots, sliced
- Olive oil
- Maple syrup
- ¼ cup roasted pumpkin seeds
- 1 lime
- Basil

For the Butternut Squash

Preheat a water bath to 183°F (83.9°C).

Peel the squash then cut in half and remove the seeds. Cut the flesh into ½" (13mm) chunks. You should have about 2 cups.

Place the cubed squash in one or two sous vide bags, making sure it is in a single layer. Add the garlic, ginger, red curry paste, and butter to the sous vide bag. Seal the bag and cook for at least an hour, but preferably 2 to 4.

Once cooked, remove the squash from the sous vide bag and place in a blender or food processor. Add the lime juice, vegetable broth, coconut milk, salt and pepper then blend until fully pureed.

To Assemble

Saute the shallots in a pan with olive oil until they brown and begin to get crispy. Remove from the heat and pat dry.

Place a ladle or two of the soup in a bowl then drizzle with maple syrup. Sprinkle some roasted pumpkin seeds on top, top with the shallots, zest some lime over the soup and add a thai basil leaf or two then serve.

Chipotle Sweet Potato Salad

Cooks: 183°F (83.9°C) for 45 to 60 minutes • Serves: 4 as a side

This sweet potato salad is a fun twist on the ubiquitous potato salad served at picnics everywhere. The sweet potatoes are cooked with a flavorful spice mixture and then combined with corn and black beans before being topped with a spicy chipotle vinaigrette.

Sweet potatoes normally take about 30 to 60 minutes to tenderize, depending on how tender you want them and the size of the pieces. For this recipe we cut them all into cubes so the cooking time usually evens out to 45 minutes.

For the Sweet Potatoes
- 4 sweet potatoes
- 4 tablespoons butter
- 2 teaspoons ground coriander
- 1 teaspoon ground cumin
- 1 teaspoon ancho chile powder
- 1 teaspoon kosher salt
- 1 teaspoon ground cloves
- ½ teaspoon black pepper

For the Vinaigrette
- 1 chipotle chile from a can of chipotles in adobo
- 1 garlic clove, finely minced
- 2 tablespoons ketchup
- 6 tablespoons lime juice
- 1 tablespoon honey
- ½ cup olive oil

To Assemble
- 2 tablespoons olive oil
- 3 shallots, diced
- 2 cups corn kernels, cooked
- 2 cups canned black beans, rinsed and drained
- ½ cup chopped cilantro

For the Sweet Potatoes
Preheat the water bath to 183°F (83.9°C).

Peel the sweet potatoes and cut into ¾" to 1" (19mm to 25mm) chunks. Add them to the sous vide bag in a single layer along with the butter and the spices then seal. Cook for 45 to 60 minutes until the potatoes are soft.

For the Vinaigrette
Put the chipotle, garlic and ketchup in a blender and process until smooth. Add the lime juice, honey, salt and pepper, and process again. Slowly add the olive oil while processing until it is incorporated. The vinaigrette can be refrigerated for several hours and re-whisked before serving.

To Assemble
Heat the olive oil in a pan over medium heat. Add the shallots and heat for 5 minutes. Add the corn and beans and heat through. Remove from the heat.

Remove the sweet potatoes from the sous vide bag and place in a serving bowl. Add the shallots, corn, beans, and cilantro and toss to combine. Spoon the dressing over the salad and toss once more before serving.

Apple Bourbon-Maple Chutney

185°F (85°C) for 90 to 120 minutes • Serves: 8 as a topping

This apple chutney is a very flavorful topping that works great on pork or fish. Sometimes I'll even use it as a savory topping on desserts. The apples are cooked in a bourbon, maple syrup, chipotle and thyme mixture. After a brief puree they are ready to go. For a thicker chutney, or if the apples release too many juices, they can be briefly simmered before pureeing them to reduce the juices down. You can leave the skin on or peel them for a more refined presentation.

Depending on your final use of the apples, they can be cooked for anywhere between 1 to 3 hours. For this recipe I do 1.5 to 2 hours at 185°F (85°C) so they still have some bite to them.

For the Apple Chutney

- 2 Braeburn or other baking apple, diced
- 3 tablespoons bourbon
- 2 tablespoons maple syrup
- 1 tablespoon thyme leaves
- 1 tablespoon lemon juice
- 1 tablespoon melted butter
- ½ teaspoon chipotle chile powder
- Salt and pepper

For the Apple Chutney

Preheat the water bath to 185°F (85°C).

Place the apples in a sous vide bag, trying to keep the thickness of the bag less than 1" (25mm) for even cooking. Whisk together the remaining ingredients then pour over the apples. Seal the sous vide bag and cook for 90 to 120 minutes.

Once cooked, briefly blend the apple mixture to create a thick puree then serve.

Blueberry Compote

Cooks: 183°F (83.9°C) for 30 to 60 minutes • Serves: 4 as a topping

Fruit compotes, jams, and marmalades are real easy to make with sous vide. Simply put some fruit, with any pits or inedible skin removed, in a bag with some sugar and acid then cook it up to an hour or two and you are good to go.

For a thicker jam you can also throw in some pectin as well. You can make these either in sous vide bags or in filled Mason jars, but note that the end result needs to be refrigerated and can't be stored in your cabinet.

For the Blueberry Compote
8 oz blueberries (225 grams)
Zest of 1 lemon
Zest of 1 orange
⅛ teaspoon cinnamon
1 tablespoon honey

For the bourbony Compote

Preheat a water bath to 183°F (83.9°C).

Combine all the ingredients in a sous vide bag and seal. Cook for 30 to 60 minutes.

Once cooked, remove the blueberry compote from the sous vide bag and serve.

Infusions

Using sous vide to make infusions was something that took me a while to get startd with, but once I did, I started to do it all the time!

There's a lot of uses for infusions, from making flavored vinegar and oil to alcohols, syrups and specialty cocktails.

Benefits of Sous Vide Infusions

The biggest benefit to using sous vide to make an infusion is the speed it happens. In a traditional infusion, you may have to soak the flavoring agents for days, or sometimes months, to get the flavor you are looking for. With sous vide, this process can be done in a few hours.

You also have complete control over the infusion temperature, which allows you to extract different flavors into your infusions. Something infused at 130°F (54.4°C) will have a different flavor profile than when it is infused at 185°F (85°C).

If you are interested in learning a lot more information about infusions, I wrote an entire cookbook all about them. It's called *Modernist Cooking Made Easy: Infusions* and it covers making traditional infusions as well as sous vide and whipping siphon infusions.

How to Infuse with Sous Vide

The sous vide infusion process is pretty simple. Combine a liquid you want to infuse, such as alcohol, vinegar, oil, or water with some flavoring agents like herbs, spices, or fruits. I generally combine them in a Mason jar, but bags work as well.

Place the infusion in a water bath, usually set to between 131°F and 176°F (55°C and 80°C). Let the infusion cook for about 1 to 3 hours, or up to 12 hours for some oil infusions.

Once cooked, remove the infusion from the water bath and chill it completely. Strain the infusion and it is ready to use.

I was really surprised how forgiving many of the sous vide infusions were. While most of my recipes needed tweaking, the majority of them started off with really tasty outcomes. So don't hesitate to experiment with different ingredients that sound good to you, I'm sure you'll love the results!

How to Use Infused Alcohols

I recently finished my book *Modernist Cooking Made Easy: Infusions* and while it was a really fun book to work on, I did end up with more infused alcohols, vinegars and oils than I knew what to do with! I gave a lot of them away to my friends and family, but one of the uses I enjoyed most was incorporating them in cocktails. I thought I'd share some of what I've learned, some of which is also in my Infusions book.

Ways to Use Infused Alcohols

I try to keep it simple when creating cocktails using infused spirits and usually turn to recipes that will showcase the infusion while subtly complementing it. I tend to stick to variations of traditional cocktails that are easy to tweak, letting the infusion shine.

Neat, Up, On the Rocks, or With a Twist

It's not technically a cocktail, but serving an infusion straight up is the easiest way to highlight its flavor. You can do this chilled or unchilled, depending on the liquor you are enjoying. Serving it over ice helps to water it down and let the flavors stand out from the harshness of the alcohol. Adding a twist of citrus peel, a mint leaf, or another garnish can help round out the flavors.

When I first make an infusion I always try it neat, as well as on the rocks. From there I can decide which way I want to go with the cocktail I'll be making.

Classic Cocktails

I tend to focus on simple cocktails that use only a few ingredients. This allows me to more easily enjoy the infusion without having to control too many variables. I love to try this with many of my favorites like the Manhattan, martini, Old Fashioned, Paloma, margarita and several other classics.

Because I make these drinks a lot, it has become relatively easy for me to replace the alcohol with a flavored infusion and really enjoy the nuance it adds. Tweaking the mixer or the bitters to go with the new infusion also helps the drinks come together.

The Tasting Flight

Several of my friends enjoy trying different infusions and the cocktails using them. To really showcase the infusion I'll often set up a tasting flight for them. I'll serve a ½ ounce shot of the unflavored spirit, a 1 ounce shot of the infusion, either neat or on the rocks, and a cocktail containing that infusion. This allows them to taste the full spectrum of the changes the infusion creates.

New, Composed Cocktails

Finally, there are many wonderfully subtle and unique cocktails that talented bartenders are putting together using infusions. I, like most people, do not have the palate or mixing experience to create these myself, so over the years I've learned to stick to what is simple. If you like the more nuanced and elaborate cocktails I recommend looking at some online bar menus such as from The Dead Rabbit[21], Blueprint[22], or any of the amazing cocktail bars that will get you going in the right direction. I also have several great recommendations for cocktail books[23] I've found that present unique concepts or further discuss the process of building complex cocktails.

Strawberry Basil Infused Rum

Cooks: 131°F (55°C) for 1 to 3 hours

This recipe highlights a simple alcohol infusion. I kept the temperature low to preserve the brightness of the basil and strawberries, but for other ingredients you can go higher.

This infusion always reminds me of early summer, eating ripe strawberries and sitting on the deck. The basil adds a nice hint of spice to the infusion. This rum goes great in mojitos and rum punch but I really like it in a fizz to cool me off on a warm summer day.

For the Strawberry Basil Rum
- 7 large strawberries
- 15 basil leaves
- 1.5 cups rum

For the Strawberry Basil Rum

Preheat a water bath to 131°F (55.0°C).

Coarsely chop the strawberries and basil. Combine the strawberries, basil, and rum in a sous vide bag or Mason jar then seal and place in the water bath. Heat the infusion for 1 to 3 hours.

Prepare an ice bath with ½ ice and ½ water. Remove the bag or Mason jar from the water bath and place in the ice bath for 15 to 20 minutes. Strain the rum and store in a sealed container.

Citrus Infused Oil

Cooks: 150°F (65.5°C) for 1 to 2 hours

Capturing the nuanced flavors of citrus zest in oil is an excellent way to quickly add it to various dishes. You can use any combination of citrus, depending on what is in season in your area. I normally use a blend of the neutral tasting grapeseed oil with some olive oil to round out the flavors, but whatever oil you have on hand will work great.

For the Citrus Infused Oil
1 lime
1 orange
1 lemon
½ grapefruit
1 cup grapeseed oil
½ cup olive oil

For the Citrus Infused Oil

Preheat a water bath to 150°F (65.5°C).

Lightly scrub the outside of the citrus then remove the zest with a vegetable peeler or zester. Make sure little to no pith came off as well, using a paring knife to remove any.

Combine all of the ingredients in a sous vide bag or Mason jar then seal. Infuse in the water bath for 1 to 2 hours.

Prepare an ice bath with ½ ice and ½ water. Remove the bag or jar from the water bath and place in the ice bath for 15 to 20 minutes. Strain the oil and store in a sealed container. It will last for a week or two in the refrigerator.

Cherry Vanilla Balsamic Vinegar

Cooks: 140°F (60°C) for 1 to 2 hours

Vinegar infusions work very similarly to alcohol infusions. I bump the temperature up some here to pull out more flavor from the cherries and vanilla.

The sweet and tart cherry flavor goes wonderfully with the taste of earthy vanilla. They are both strong flavors and can hold up well to balsamic vinegar, increasing the already deep flavors found there. If you want a vinegar where the cherry and vanilla flavors shine more brightly try using a white balsamic or white wine vinegar instead.

For the Cherry Vanilla Vinegar
15 cherries
1 vanilla bean, split lengthwise
1.5 cups balsamic vinegar

For the Cherry Vanilla Vinegar
Preheat a water bath to 140°F (60.0°C).

Remove the stems from the cherries, you can leave the pits in or remove them, and place in a sous vide bag or Mason jar. Lightly crush or muddle the cherries. Add the vanilla bean to the cherries. Pour the vinegar over top then seal and place in the water bath. Heat the infusion for 1 to 2 hours.

Prepare an ice bath with ½ ice and ½ water. Remove the bag or Mason jar from the water bath and place in the ice bath for 15 to 20 minutes. Strain the vinegar and store in a sealed container.

Eggs

Sous vide eggs are one of the things I struggle most with. I've had some really good results and some mediocre results, and I'm not always sure what went wrong. I'm also generally good at making eggs in traditional ways so I tend not to reach for the sous vide machine as much. That said, here's some of the egg-making information I've found to be consistently good.

The first thing to realize is that eggs actually contain three parts and these three parts all cook differently, are best at different temperatures and cook at different speeds. The parts are the yolk, the tight white contained in the membrane, and the loose white outside the membrane. These three parts are why there is so much variability in how you cook eggs, and why the precision control of sous vide can be valuable.

What to Sous Vide Eggs In?

The first question people almost always ask is what they need to put their eggs in to sous vide them.

Most people simply put their eggs in the water bath with no container around them except for the shell. This works well as long as one doesn't break, which could result in your machine getting gummed up and needing a cleaning.

Some people put them in a Ziploc bag just to be safe in case they break.

If you remove the eggs from the shell, you can cook them in Mason jars, ramekins, or vacuum bags. You can also put the eggs in plastic wrap, which when heated turns them into almost flower-like shapes.

What Temperature to Sous Vide Eggs At?

Because of the three parts of the egg, they are very finicky and even a degree or two can result in a large change in texture. For a great look at egg temperatures I recommend either the Chef Steps online calculator[24] or the Serious Eats Guide to Sous Vide-Style Eggs[25].

"Raw" Pasteurized Eggs

From 130°F to 135°F (54.4°C to 57.2°C) the egg will remain "raw" and if it is held at this temperature for at least 75 to 90 minutes it will be fully pasteurized and safe to eat. It can then safely be used in place of raw eggs in preparations such as mayonnaise, cookie dough, or salad dressings.

Soft Boiled and Poached Eggs

The soft boiled or poached range is about 140°F to 145°F (60°C to 62.8°C) and the eggs are cooked for 45 to 60 minutes. For a firmer white without affecting the texture of the yolk, the egg can be briefly boiled for 2 to 3 minutes either before or after the sous vide process. This will also help with removing the shell from the eggs.

Eggs cooked at this temperature can be chilled and refrigerated, or held at 130°F (54.4°C) without changing the texture.

For a cleaner presentation of poached or soft boiled eggs you can gently crack them into a small bowl and then use a slotted spoon to remove the egg. This will leave the runny loose white behind. The eggs can also be briefly poached in boiling water once they have been removed from the shell for a more traditional poached look.

Semi Hard and Hard Boiled Eggs

At 150°F (65.6°C) the yolk begins to firm up until it becomes crumbly around 165°F (73.9°C). Hard boiled eggs start in the middle of this range, though I still prefer to use the traditional boil in a pot method for them.

13 Minute Egg on Wilted Spinach

Cooks: 167°F (75°C) for 13 minutes • Serves: 4

The 13 minute egg is one of the most popular ways to cook eggs because it's easy, fast, and the results are really great. I first heard of the 13 minute eggs from Ideas in Food but many other chefs use this technique as well. The timing in this recipe is critical because of the high heat, it's one of the rare sous vide recipes where you are not trying to bring the food up to the temperature of the water bath. The high temperature cooks the whites of the egg much more than the yolks, leaving a runny yolk with a firmer white.

For the Eggs
4 Eggs

For the Wilted Spinach Salad
8 cups baby spinach
4 strips bacon, cut into batons
2 shallots, diced
4 garlic cloves, minced
3 tablespoons lemon juice

To Assemble
Basil, minced
Parmesan cheese for grating
Lemon quarters

For the Eggs
Preheat a water bath to 167°F (75°C).

Gently place the eggs in the water bath and let cook for 13 minutes. Once cooked, remove from the water bath and set aside.

For the Wilted Spinach Salad
Place the spinach in a bowl and set aside.

Heat the bacon over medium heat until the fat has rendered and the bacon is crispy, 15 to 20 minutes. Remove and discard all but about 1 tablespoon of the bacon fat. Add the shallots and garlic, cook until the shallots turn translucent, 3 to 5 minutes. Stir in the lemon juice then pour the mixture over the spinach and toss well to combine. Salt and pepper to taste.

To Assemble
Place some spinach in a bowl, leaving an indentation at the top to hold the egg. Crack a 13 minute egg over the top of the spinach, sprinkle with the basil, then grate the parmesan cheese on top. Squeeze some lemon juice over the dish then serve.

Egg Cup Bites

Cooks: 170°F (76.6°C) for 1 hour • Serves: 4

These egg cup bites were first popularized by Starbucks but are really easy to make at home. You can use any ingredients you want to flavor them but my favorite is broccoli, cheddar cheese and bacon. For a lighter egg you can replace the cream with milk, or use ¼ cup cream cheese for a denser egg.

You can make them in any glass container but the ¼ pint or ½ pint work really well. I've also made them in ramekins which create a great shape for the egg.

For the Eggs
6 Eggs
½ cup shredded cheddar cheese
½ cup heavy cream
½ cup dice cooked broccoli
½ cup crumbled cooked bacon
½ cup cooked shallots

For the Eggs
Preheat a water bath to 170°F (76.6°C).

Whisk or blend together the eggs, cheese and cream. Stir in the broccoli, bacon, and shallots. Pour into 4 Mason jars and finger tighten the lids. Place in the water bath and cook for 60 minutes.

Remove from the water bath and serve by running a knife along the inside of the jar.

Dairy, Grains and More

Even though sous vide is usually used to cook meat and vegetables, at the most basic level it just excels at holding something at a set temperature.

This ability can be used to easily prepare items that need to be held at constant temperatures, such as yogurt, cheese, custards, and some egg preparations like lemon curd. It also works well for many types of grains, incuding oatmeal, quinoa, farro, and many rices.

Most of the these types of dishes are cooked in Mason jars or ramekins.

When using ramekins the level of the water is always lower than the lip of the container. If you need to use deeper water, you can often place the ramekins on a wire rack to keep them out of the water.

Mason jars can be placed directly in the water with the lid hand tightened so bubbles can escape if the buildup of pressure becomes too great.

But don't limit yourself to the usual. Because of the constantly held temperatures some people have used sous vide to temper chocolate, decrystalize honey, steep expensive tea, brew beer, as a circulated bath for keeping beer and wine cold, to develop film and even a foot soaking bath!

Cinnamon-Vanilla Crème Brulee

Cooks: 190°F (87.8°C) for 60 to 90 minutes • Serves: 4

Most people think creme brulee is a real fancy dish but it's actually very simple to make. Using a sous vide machine makes it even easier. This is a classic creme brulee and you can take it in a variety of directions depending on the flavors you want.

To get the ramekins at the proper height it is helpful to put a bowl or strainer upside down in the water bath and place a plate or sheet pan on top of it where the ramekins can sit. If you have a lid for your water bath make sure you use it, it will keep the air hot as well as eliminate evaporation, otherwise be sure to maintain the water level throughout the cooking process.

The best depth for the creme brulee is usually less than an inch (25mm) deep, otherwise the inside might not cook all the way through. For deeper creme brulees you may need to increase the cooking time to offset the depth. If your ramekins are touching each other in the water bath it can help to rotate them half way through the cooking process to ensure they cook evenly.

For the Creme Brulee
2 cups heavy or whipping cream
1 vanilla bean
1 cinnamon stick
4 egg yolks
Pinch of salt
⅓ cup white sugar

To Assemble
Sugar
Mint leaves

For the Creme Brulee

Place an upside down strainer or bowl in your water bath. Top with a sheet pan or plate. Set the ramekins on it and fill the water bath two-thirds of the way up the ramekin. Preheat the water bath to 190°F (87.8°C).

Pour the heavy cream into a pot. Split the vanilla bean and scrape out the seeds, add the seeds and the bean to the cream. Add the cinnamon stick. Bring just to a simmer, stirring regularly. Turn off the heat and let it infuse for 10 minutes. Strain the cream.

Whisk together the egg yolks in another bowl then slowly whisk in the salt and sugar, the mixture should turn glossy and thicken slightly. Slowly whisk in the infused cream. Evenly divide among the ramekins, cover each ramekin with plastic wrap and use a rubber band to hold it in place. Place the ramekins in the sous vide bath with the water level coming two thirds of the way up the side. Cook for 60 to 90 minutes, depending on how thick you prefer your creme brulee.

Once cooked, remove from the water bath and let cool for 15 to 20 minutes. Place in the refrigerator and chill until cold, or preferably overnight.

To Assemble

Spread a thin layer of sugar a few grains thick on the top of the creme brulee and quickly torch until the sugar melts and begins to brown. Add a few mint leaves then serve.

Sous Vide Yogurt

Cooks: 110°F (43.3°C) for 5 hours • Serves: 4 cups yogurt

To make yogurt you heat milk or cream to above 180°F (82.2°C), cool it down and mix with a starter culture, then let it incubate at 100°F to 120°F (37.8°C to 48.9°C) for several hours. Using a sous vide machine allows you to easily maintain the temperatures you are looking for.

Sous vide yogurt is typically made in glass Mason jars with the lids either off or not fully tightened. The starter bacteria will give off gasses as they create the yogurt so a sealed container can leak or explode. The yogurt is also usually made in the container you will store or serve it from because moving it to a new one can affect the consistency of the yogurt.

You can use the sous vide machine to reach both temperatures but I typically just heat the milk on the stove because it's much quicker than raising and lowering the temperature of the whole water bath.

I call for half and half, which results in a very thick yogurt. If you prefer a thinner one you can substitute whole or 2% milk. To get the incubation going you need to add a ½ cup of yogurt that contains live and active cultures. Yogurt that contains this type of culture will be labelled on the package. The length of the incubation time adds tanginess to the yogurt and can range from 3 hours to 24 hours.

For the Yogurt

4 cups half and half or milk
½ cup plain yogurt with live and active cultures

For the Yogurt

Fill a water bath to about an inch (25mm) below the height of the Mason jars you are using and preheat the water to 110°F (43.3°C).

Heat the half and half in a pot to at least 180°F (82.2°C). Remove it from the heat and let it cool to at least 120°F (48.9°C) then whisk in the yogurt with the live and active cultures. Pour the mixture into the Mason jars and seal each with plastic wrap. Place the jars in the water bath and let incubate for 5 hours.

After 5 hours remove the jars from the water bath and refrigerate until chilled. Once the yogurt is cold, seal with the Mason jar lids. It will last in the refrigerator for 1 to 2 weeks.

Equipment Links

There are several different kinds of equipment you can use in sous vide, and each kind has many different brands that are offering solutions. Here are some of my favorite brands broken down by category. The equipment used in sous vide is constantly evolving so I highly recommend checking out my online sous vide equipment pages at http://AFMEasy.com/SVEquip for all the latest details.

Searing

Once your food is cooked you need to get a great sear on it. Here are a few of the top options for accomplishing that.

Bernzomatic
Bernzomatic is the generally considered the best torch to sear sous vide food with.
www.bernzomatic.com
amzn.to/2lDsajY

Iwatani Torch
Iwatani also makes a high quality torch for searing sous vide food.
www.iwatani.com
amzn.to/2li8K8j

Searzall
The Searzall is an attachment for the Bernzomatic torch that allows for more even, gentle heating.
www.bookeranddax.com
amzn.to/2m0koBD

Lodge Cast Iron Skillet
A good cast iron skillet is great for searing, or to use as a base for torching your food.
www.lodgemfg.com
amzn.to/2lij4gm

All-Clad Stainless Steel Fry Pan
A good, heavy stainless steel frying pan is also a wonderful way to sear your food.
www.all-clad.com
amzn.to/2mxpus8

Circulators

Immersion circulators and water baths are the backbone of sous vide. They keep the water at a set temperature and ensure your food will turn out perfectly.

Joule
The Joule is a WiFi-enabled sous vide circulator by ChefSteps that can only be controlled via a smartphone app.
www.chefsteps.com/joule
amzn.to/2ke8zX5

Sansaire
The Sansaire is a first generation circulator that is powerful and quiet.
www.sansaire.com
amzn.to/2jUCBhf

Anova
The Anova is one of the best selling sous vide circulators and comes with or without WiFi.
www.anovaculinary.com
amzn.to/2m0pfTH

Gourmia
Gourmia is a less expensive, but powerful, circulator that can also come with WiFi.
www.gourmia.com
amzn.to/2lgIdDI

Containers, Clips and Racks

There are a wide variety of containers you can use for sous vide, as well as clips and racks that help hold your food in place during the long cook times.

Cambro Container
Cambro makes several sizes of polycarbonate containers that are excellent for sous vide.
www.cambro.com
amzn.to/2lDL4Hv

Rubbermaid Container
Rubbermaid also makes several sizes of containers that work well for sous vide.
www.rubbermaid.com
amzn.to/2lDGgC0

Lipavi Container
Lipavi has a full line of containers and matching racks, along with cut lids for many circulators.
www.lipavi.com
amzn.to/2mxz66n

Uxcell Alligator Clamp
These clips are a convenient way to keep your sous vide bag attached to the container.
www.uxcell.com
amzn.to/2lE1ek4

CMS Disc Magnet
These strong magnets are a great way to hold your sous vide bags in place.
www.cmsmagnetics.com
amzn.to/2lxJgiy

Sous Vide Magnets
These magnets are silicon coated and made specifically for sous vide machines.
amzn.to/2nbr96H

Sous Vide Supreme Rack
This inexpensive rack made by Sous Vide Supreme works great in many other containers as well.
www.sousvidesupreme.com
bit.ly/2mPhvG0

Ikea Variera Rack
IKEA makes a dish holder rack that many people use in their sous vide machines to hold down their bags.
www.ikea.com
amzn.to/2mKmO7I

Sealers

There are three common ways to seal a sous vide bag. They are with a chambered vacuum sealer, an "edge-type" vacuum sealer, and a Ziploc bag.

FoodSaver
FoodSaver is the best selling edge-style vacuum sealer on the market and has many different models at multiple price points.
www.foodsaver.com
amzn.to/2lYkPOq

VacMaster
VacMaster makes several chambered vacuum sealers which are expensive but are excellent for sous vide and general food storage.
www.vacmaster.com
amzn.to/2m0rYfT

Oliso
The Oliso vacuum sealer is similar to a FoodSaver but is more compact.
www.oliso.com/shop/vacuumsealer

Ziploc
Ziploc bags are in almost everyone's kitchen and are an inexpensive way to seal food for sous vide.
ziploc.com
amzn.to/2lYx3GU

Other

Here are a few other cooking accessories I like to use or mention in the book. Some are for everyday cooking and others are great for special occasions.

PolyScience Smoking Gun
The Smoking Gun is an excellent way to add flavor and aroma to many dishes.
www.polyscience.com
amzn.to/2lDJVji

Fagor Pressure Cooker
A good pressure cooker is a great way to quickly make braise-like food.
www.fagoramerica.com
amzn.to/2lnyz6T

iSi Gourmet Whip
A whipping siphon is one of my favorite kitchen tools and is wonderful for infusions, whipped cream, and foams.
www.isi.com/us/culinary
amzn.to/2mOSMzr

Cooking by Thickness

There are two ways to cook sous vide, one is based on the thickness of the food and the other is based on the desired tenderness. When cooking based on the thickness of the food it is helpful to have a reference guide to fall back on. I've combined several of the respectable sous vide charts into one easy-to-use reference. Both methods have their uses. Thickness-based is great for very tender cuts cooked by people who need them done in the minimum amount of time. Tenderness-based is best for tougher cuts or people that have a range of time that they are interested in. This chapter focuses on thickness and the next is on tenderness.

Cooking By Thickness

Cooking sous vide based on thickness basically tells you the minimum time you can cook a piece of meat to ensure it is safe and comes up to temperature in the middle. It doesn't take in to account tenderizing time or any other factors.

Cooking based on thickness is how PolyScience, Baldwin, and Nathan started out as they did research on food safety.

Cooking by thickness is most often used by restaurants or home cooks who want to minimize cooking time and are using tender cuts of meat that don't need any tenderization.

Notes on the Thickness Times

The times were extrapolated from the descriptions in Baldwin's *Practical Guide to Sous Vide*[26] as well as Nathan's tables on eGullet[27] and a few other sources.

The times given are approximate since there are many factors that go in to how quickly food is heated. The density of the food matters a lot, which is one reason beef heats differently than chicken. To a lesser degree where you get your beef from will also affect the cooking time, and whether the beef was factory raised, farm raised, or grass-fed. Because of this, I normally don't try to pull the food out at the exact minute it is done unless I'm in a real rush.

The times shown are also the minimum times to heat or pasteurize the food. The food can be, and sometimes needs to be, left in for longer periods in order to fully tenderize the meat. If you are cooking food longer, remember that food should not be cooked at temperatures less than 131°F (55°C) for more than 4 hours.

For a printable version of these charts you can download the ruler from my website at: www.AFMEasy.com/Ruler.

Thickness Times for Beef, Lamb and Pork

These are the times for heating, cooling, and pasteurizing beef, lamb and other red meat, as well as pork. These times apply to most types of meat except fish, though chicken and poultry are almost always cooked to pasteurization and have been moved to their own section for clarity. If you have some other type of meat (moose, bear, rabbit, etc.) you can use these charts as well.

Heating Times for Beef, Lamb and Pork

These times specify how long it takes a piece of meat, with a particular shape, to heat all the way to the center. The center of the meat will come up to about 1° less than the water bath temperature in the time given. The final degree takes a much longer time and generally does not contribute to the final taste or texture.

While there are slight differences in the heating time for different temperatures of water baths, the times usually vary less than 5 to 10% even going from a 111°F bath to a 141°F bath (43.8°C to 60.5°C), which equates to a difference of 5 minutes every hour. I show the largest value in the chart.

Remember that you should not cook food at much less than 130°F (54.5°C) for more than 4 hours. If you want to cook a piece of food at a lower temperature, you can cut it into smaller portions so it heats more quickly. The times shown are also minimum times and food can be, and sometimes needs to be, left in for longer periods in order to fully tenderize it.

Starting Temp: Shape of Meat:	Fridge Slab	Fridge Cylinder	Freezer Slab	Freezer Cylinder
2.75" (70mm)	–	3:30	–	5:00
2.50" (63mm)	5:10	2:50	–	4:20
2.25" (57mm)	4:25	2:20	6:35	3:45
2.00" (51mm)	3:35	2:00	5:30	3:00
1.75" (44mm)	3:00	1:30	4:30	2:30
1.50" (38mm)	2:20	1:10	3:20	1:50
1.25" (32mm)	1:40	0:55	2:35	1:20
1.00" (25mm)	1:15	0:40	1:50	1:00
0.75" (19mm)	0:50	0:30	1:15	0:45
0.50" (13mm)	0:30	0:15	0:40	0:25
0.25" (6mm)	0:10	0:06	0:15	0:15

Pasteurization Times for Beef, Lamb and Pork

If you want to ensure that your food is safe to eat through pasteurization, then you can follow these sous vide times. They let you know how long you need to cook something, specifically most red meat, for it to be effectively pasteurized and safe to eat.

Like the heating and cooling times, they are not exact, but they are also on the longer side for safety reasons.

Thickness	131°F (55°C)	135°F (57°C)	140°F (60°C)
2.75" (70mm)	6:30	5:15	4:00
2.50" (63mm)	5:40	4:35	3:35
2.25" (57mm)	5:10	4:00	3:05
2.00" (51mm)	4:30	3:20	2:30
1.75" (44mm)	4:00	3:00	2:15
1.50" (38mm)	3:25	2:25	1:55
1.25" (32mm)	3:10	2:05	1:40
1.00" (25mm)	2:45	2:00	1:30
0.75" (19mm)	2:30	1:45	1:15
0.50" (13mm)	2:10	1:25	0:50
0.25" (6mm)	1:50	1:00	0:35

Cooling Times for Beef, Lamb and Pork

If you are cooking food and then storing it in the refrigerator or freezer, then these sous vide cooling times will give you the time that food needs to be in an ice bath before the center is chilled out of the danger zone.

Just like with heating, the actual temperature change isn't a big factor in the time needed to cool it. Just make sure the ice bath is at least one half ice to ensure proper cooling.

Starting Temp: Shape of Meat:	Hot Cylinder	Hot Slab
2.75" (70mm)	2:45	5:30
2.50" (63mm)	2:10	4:35
2.25" (57mm)	1:50	4:00
2.00" (51mm)	1:30	3:15
1.75" (44mm)	1:15	2:45
1.50" (38mm)	1:00	2:05
1.25" (32mm)	0:45	1:35
1.00" (25mm)	0:30	1:15
0.75" (19mm)	0:20	0:50
0.50" (13mm)	0:15	0:30
0.25" (6mm)	0:10	0:15

Thickness Times for Chicken and Poultry

Sous vide chicken is almost always cooked until it is pasteurized. For heating and cooling times you can reference the previous section.

Pasteurization Times for Chicken

The sous vide pasteurization times in the chart will ensure that the chicken is always safe to eat. These times are for chicken that has been in the refrigerator, for frozen chicken add some extra time.

Thickness	137°F (58°C)	140°F (60°C)	145°F (63°C)	149°F (65°C)
2.75" (70mm)	6:00	5:00	4:15	3:45
2.50" (63mm)	5:20	4:25	3:35	3:10
2.25" (57mm)	4:50	4:05	3:10	2:55
2.00" (51mm)	4:15	3:20	2:30	2:20
1.75" (44mm)	3:45	3:00	2:15	2:00
1.50" (38mm)	3:10	2:30	1:55	1:40
1.25" (32mm)	2:55	2:10	1:40	1:25
1.00" (25mm)	2:15	1:35	1:15	0:55
0.75" (19mm)	2:00	1:20	0:50	0:40
0.50" (13mm)	1:50	1:10	0:35	0:25
0.25" (6mm)	1:40	0:50	0:25	0:20

Heating Times for Fatty Fish

These sous vide times will help you determine how long you need to cook fatty fish in order for it to be brought up to temperature. It will not pasteurize the fish, so make sure you use high quality fish you would be comfortable eating raw.

There are slight differences in the heating time for different temperatures of water baths but they usually vary less than 5 to 10% even going from a 111°F bath to a 141°F bath (43.8°C to 60.5°C), which equates to a difference of 5 minutes every hour. I show the largest value in the chart.

The chart assumes the fish is defrosted.

Thickness	Time
2.75" (70mm)	3:50
2.50" (63mm)	3:05
2.25" (57mm)	2:40
2.00" (51mm)	2:00
1.75" (44mm)	1:40
1.50" (38mm)	1:20
1.25" (32mm)	0:55
1.00" (25mm)	0:35
0.75" (19mm)	0:21
0.50" (13mm)	0:10
0.25" (6mm)	0:05

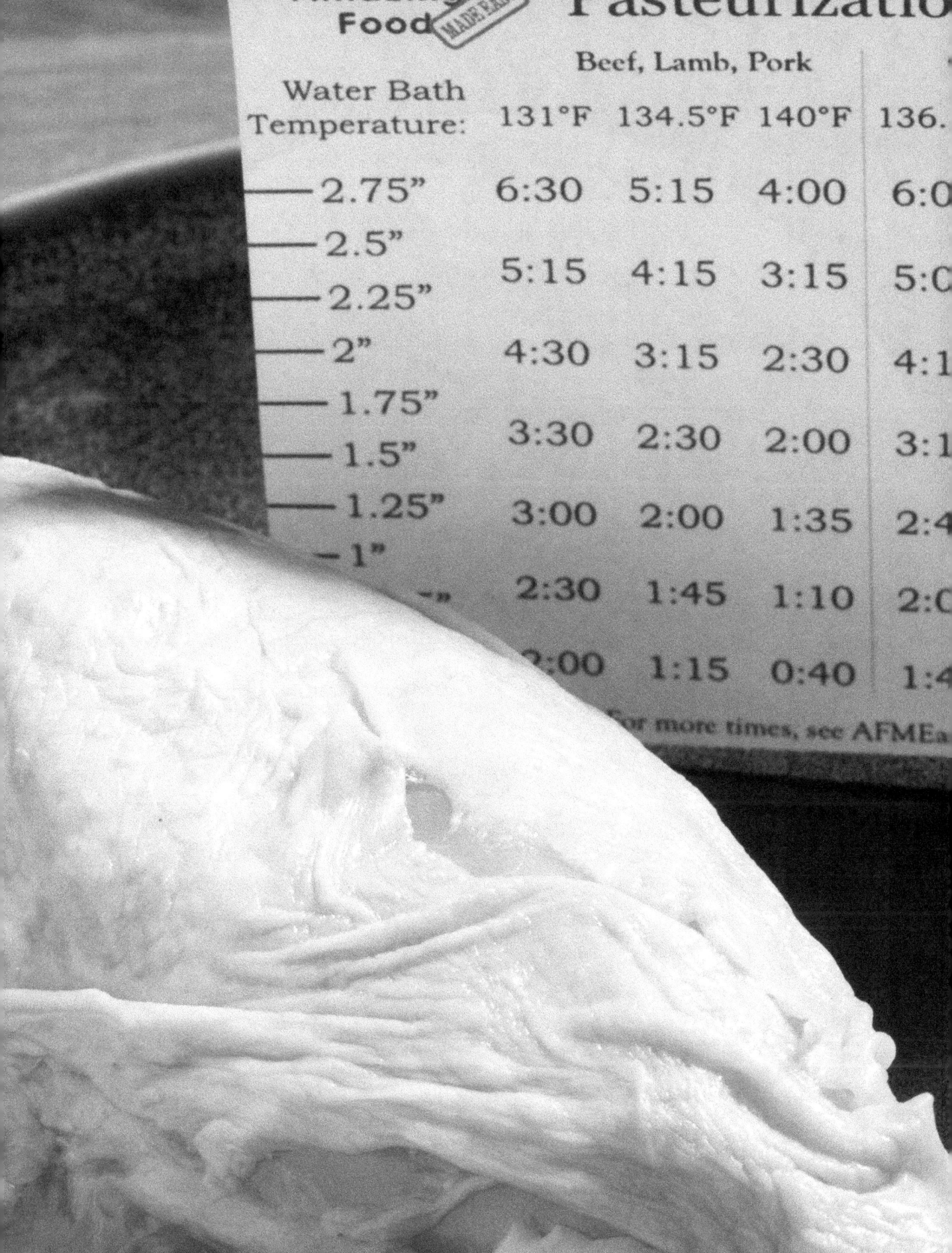

Cooking By Tenderness

Cooking by tenderness is dependent on how tender or tough the cut of meat is. Some cuts just need to be heated through while others need extended cooks of several days until they are broken down enough to enjoy.

To come up with the tenderness times I've leaned on my own experience and the reports of other people. It is important to understand that all times are estimates, as there are many factors that go in to how tough a piece of meat is. I have cooked a chuck roast for 18 hours and had it turn out too tender, and I've cooked one for 36 hours that was still tough.

The best way to get consistent results is to turn to a butcher or fish monger that you frequent so you can understand how their meat cooks.

A lot of the times given are my personal preferences as well, if you like something cooked longer or shorter, please go with what you prefer.

Note: For more info about the ranges given, please read the Deep Look: Why the Range? section in the How Sous Vide Times Work chapter.

Beef, Pork, Lamb and Other Meat

Most of the cuts below can have a few different options including "Steak-Like", "Tender Steak" and up to three braising entries.

Steak-Like

Following the "Steak-Like" entry will result in a final dish that has the texture and doneness of a good steak. I recommend starting with 125°F (51.6°C) for rare, 131°F (55°C) for medium rare and 140°F (60°C) for medium. You can then adjust the temperature up or down in future cooks to better match your preference.

General Doneness Range
Rare: 120°F to 129°F (49°C to 53.8°C)
Medium Rare: 130°F to 139°F (54.4°C to 59.4°C)
Medium: 140°F to 145°F (60°C to 62.8°C)
Well Done: Above 145°F (62.8°C)

For the timing, you usually will be given a specific range that I've found to work well for that cut, such as "2 to 4 hours", or "1 to 2 days".

Other timing options are "Time by Thickness" or "Pasteurize by Thickness", which indicates that this cut doesn't need tenderization, it only needs to be heated through and/or pasteurized. You can follow the charts in the Cooking By Thickness chapter for the specific times. I've used "Pasteurize by Thickness" for entries that are almost always pasteurized, but many people also pasteurize the majority of their meat to be on the safe side.

> **Warning:** If you drop the temperature much below 130°F (54.4°C) you are in the danger zone, not killing any pathogens, and shouldn't cook the food for more than an hour or two.

Tender Steak

In addition to the "Steak-Like" entry, some cuts will have a "Tender Steak" entry. These are cuts that are traditionally eaten grilled or pan fried, such as flank, sirloin, or flat iron steaks but that can also benefit from some tenderization. If you follow the "Steak-Like" entry, they will turn out very similar to the traditionally cooked version, while following the "Tender Steak" entry will result in a much more tender version of that steak.

Braise-Like

Some cuts can also be traditionally braised so I give my three favorite time and temperature combinations for them as well.

Most braise-like temperatures range from around 150°F up to 185°F (65.6°C up to 85°C). The temperatures I recommend trying first are:

- 156°F (68.8°C) for a shreddable, but still firm texture
- 165°F (73.9°C) for a more fall apart texture
- 176°F (80.0°C) for a really fall apart texture

From a timing standpoint, going from 131°F to 156°F (55°C to 68.8°C) seems to cut the cook time in half. Going above 176°F (80.0°C) seems to cut it in half again.

Beef Times and Temperatures

Blade
Steak-Like: Time by Thickness
Tender Steak: Up to 10 hours

Bottom Round
Steak-Like: For 2 to 3 days
Braise-Like:
    156°F (68.8°C) for 1 to 2 days
    165°F (73.9°C) for 1 to 2 days
    176°F (80.0°C) for 12 to 24 hours

Brisket
Steak-Like: For 2 to 3 days
Braise-Like:
    156°F (68.8°C) for 1 to 2 days
    165°F (73.9°C) for 1 to 2 days
    176°F (80.0°C) for 12 to 24 hours

Cheek
Steak-Like: For 2 to 3 days
Braise-Like:
    156°F (68.8°C) for 1 to 2 days
    165°F (73.9°C) for 1 to 2 days
    176°F (80.0°C) for 12 to 24 hours

Chuck
Pot Roast
Steak-Like: For 36 to 60 hours
Braise-Like:
    156°F (68.8°C) for 18 to 24 hours
    165°F (73.9°C) for 18 to 24 hours
    176°F (80.0°C) for 12 to 18 hours

Eye Round
Steak-Like: For 1 to 2 days
Braise-Like:
    156°F (68.8°C) for 18 to 36 hours
    165°F (73.9°C) for 18 to 36 hours
    176°F (80.0°C) for 8 to 18 hours

Flank
Bavette
Steak-Like: Time by Thickness
Tender Steak: Up to 2 days, I prefer 12 hours

Flat Iron
Steak-Like: Time by Thickness
Tender Steak: Up to 24 hours

Hamburger
Steak-Like: Pasteurize by Thickness

Hanger
Steak-Like: Time by Thickness

London Broil
Not a true cut but normally flank, chuck, or round
Steak-Like: For 18 to 60 hours
Braise-Like:
    156°F (68.8°C) for 12 to 24 hours
    165°F (73.9°C) for 12 to 24 hours
    176°F (80.0°C) for 8 to 18 hours

Porterhouse
Steak-Like: Time by Thickness

Pot Roast
Steak-Like: For 2 to 3 days
Braise-Like:
    156°F (68.8°C) for 1 to 2 days
    165°F (73.9°C) for 1 to 2 days
    176°F (80.0°C) for 12 to 24 hours

Prime Rib
Standing Rib Roast, Rib Roast
Steak-Like: Time by Thickness
Tender Steak: Up to 10 hours

Ribeye
Rib Steak, Delmonico Steak, Scotch Filet, Entrecôte
Steak-Like: Time by Thickness
Tender Steak: Up to 8 hours

Ribs
Beef Spareribs
Steak-Like: For 1 to 2 days
Braise-Like:
   156°F (68.8°C) for 18 to 36 hours
   165°F (73.9°C) for 18 to 36 hours
   176°F (80.0°C) for 8 to 18 hours

Sausage
Steak-Like: Pasteurize by Thickness

Shank
Shin
Steak-Like: For 2 to 3 days
Braise-Like:
   156°F (68.8°C) for 1 to 2 days
   165°F (73.9°C) for 1 to 2 days
   176°F (80.0°C) for 12 to 24 hours

Short Ribs
Back Ribs, Flanken Ribs
Steak-Like: For 2 to 3 days
Braise-Like:
   156°F (68.8°C) for 1 to 2 days
   165°F (73.9°C) for 1 to 2 days
   176°F (80.0°C) for 12 to 24 hours

Shoulder
Steak-Like: Time by Thickness
Tender Steak: Up to 24 hours

Sirloin
Steak-Like: Time by Thickness
Tender Steak: Up to 10 hours

Skirt
Steak-Like: Time by Thickness
Tender Steak: Up to 24 hours

Stew Meat
Various Cuts
Steak-Like: For 36 to 60 hours
Braise-Like:
   156°F (68.8°C) for 18 to 24 hours
   165°F (73.9°C) for 18 to 24 hours
   176°F (80.0°C) for 12 to 18 hours

Strip
Top Loin Strip, New York Strip, Kansas City Strip, Top Sirloin, Top Loin, Shell Steak
Steak-Like: Time by Thickness

Sweetbreads
Steak-Like: Time by Thickness

T-Bone
Steak-Like: Time by Thickness

Tenderloin
Filet mignon, Châteaubriand, Tournedo
Steak-Like: Time by Thickness

Tongue
Steak-Like: For 2 to 3 days
Braise-Like:
   156°F (68.8°C) for 1 to 2 days
   165°F (73.9°C) for 1 to 2 days
   176°F (80.0°C) for 12 to 24 hours

Top Round
Steak-Like: For 1 to 2 days
Not recommended above 145°F (62.8°C)

Tri-Tip
Steak-Like: Time by Thickness
Tender Steak: Up to 24 hours

Lamb Times and Temperatures

Arm Chop
Steak-Like: For 18 to 36 hours

Blade Chop
Steak-Like: For 18 to 36 hours

Breast
Steak-Like: For 1 to 2 days
Braise-Like:
    156°F (68.8°C) for 18 to 24 hours
    165°F (73.9°C) for 18 to 24 hours
    176°F (80.0°C) for 12 to 18 hours

Leg, Bone In
Steak-Like: Time by Thickness
Tender Steak: Up to 24 hours

Leg, Boneless
Steak-Like: Time by Thickness
Tender Steak: Up to 24 hours

Loin Chops
Steak-Like: Time by Thickness

Loin Roast
Steak-Like: Time by Thickness

Loin, Boneless
Steak-Like: Time by Thickness

Neck
Steak-Like: For 2 to 3 days
Braise-Like:
    156°F (68.8°C) for 1 to 2 days
    165°F (73.9°C) for 1 to 2 days
    176°F (80.0°C) for 12 to 24 hours

Osso Buco
Steak-Like: For 1 to 2 days
Braise-Like:
    156°F (68.8°C) for 18 to 24 hours
    165°F (73.9°C) for 18 to 24 hours
    176°F (80.0°C) for 12 to 18 hours

Rack
Steak-Like: Time by Thickness

Rib Chop
Steak-Like: Time by Thickness

Ribs
Steak-Like: For 1 to 2 days
Braise-Like:
    156°F (68.8°C) for 18 to 24 hours
    165°F (73.9°C) for 18 to 24 hours
    176°F (80.0°C) for 12 to 18 hours

Shank
Steak-Like: For 1 to 2 days
Braise-Like:
    156°F (68.8°C) for 18 to 24 hours
    165°F (73.9°C) for 18 to 24 hours
    176°F (80.0°C) for 12 to 18 hours

Shoulder
Steak-Like: For 1 to 2 days
Braise-Like:
    156°F (68.8°C) for 18 to 24 hours
    165°F (73.9°C) for 18 to 24 hours
    176°F (80.0°C) for 12 to 18 hours

Tenderloin
Steak-Like: Time by Thickness

Pork Times and Temperatures

For more information about sous viding pork and boar, please refer to the Pork and Boar chapter earlier in the book. I have replaced "Steak-Like" with "Chop-Like" so it is more accurate but please refer to the "Beef and Red Meat" intro for a full description. My recommended temperatures for "Chop-Like" pork is 135°F (57.2°C), 140°F (60°C), or 145°F (62.8°C), with 140°F (60°C) being my favorite.

Arm Steak
Chop-Like: For 1 to 2 days

Baby Back Ribs
Chop-Like: For 1 to 2 days
Braise-Like:
    156°F (68.8°C) for 18 to 24 hours
    165°F (73.9°C) for 18 to 24 hours
    176°F (80.0°C) for 12 to 18 hours

Back Ribs
Chop-Like: For 1 to 2 days
Braise-Like:
    156°F (68.8°C) for 18 to 24 hours
    165°F (73.9°C) for 18 to 24 hours
    176°F (80.0°C) for 12 to 18 hours

Belly
Chop-Like: For 2 to 3 days
Braise-Like:
    156°F (68.8°C) for 1 to 2 days
    165°F (73.9°C) for 1 to 2 days
    176°F (80.0°C) for 12 to 24 hours

Blade Chops
Chop-Like: For 8 to 12 hours

Blade Roast
Chop-Like: For 1 to 2 days
Braise-Like:
    156°F (68.8°C) for 18 to 24 hours
    165°F (73.9°C) for 18 to 24 hours
    176°F (80.0°C) for 12 to 18 hours

Blade Steak
Chop-Like: For 18 to 36 hours

Boston Butt
Chop-Like: For 1 to 2 days
Braise-Like:
    156°F (68.8°C) for 18 to 24 hours
    165°F (73.9°C) for 18 to 24 hours
    176°F (80.0°C) for 12 to 18 hours

Butt Roast
Chop-Like: For 1 to 2 days
Braise-Like:
    156°F (68.8°C) for 18 to 24 hours
    165°F (73.9°C) for 18 to 24 hours
    176°F (80.0°C) for 12 to 18 hours

Country Style Ribs
Chop-Like: For 18 to 36 hours
Braise-Like:
    156°F (68.8°C) for 9 to 18 hours
    165°F (73.9°C) for 6 to 14 hours
    176°F (80.0°C) for 4 to 9 hours

Fresh Side Pork
Chop-Like: For 2 to 3 days
Braise-Like:
    156°F (68.8°C) for 1 to 2 days
    165°F (73.9°C) for 1 to 2 days
    176°F (80.0°C) for 12 to 24 hours

Ground Pork
Pasteurize by Thickness

Ham Roast
Chop-Like: For 10 to 20 hours

Ham Steak
Chop-Like: Time by Thickness

Leg (Fresh Ham)
Chop-Like: For 10 to 20 hours

Loin Chop
Chop-Like: Pasteurize by Thickness

Loin Roast
Chop-Like: Pasteurize by Thickness

Picnic Roast
Chop-Like: For 1 to 2 days
Braise-Like:
   156°F (68.8°C) for 18 to 24 hours
   165°F (73.9°C) for 18 to 24 hours
   176°F (80.0°C) for 12 to 18 hours

Pork Chops
Chop-Like: Pasteurize by Thickness

Rib Chops
Chop-Like: For 5 to 8 hours

Rib Roast
Chop-Like: For 5 to 8 hours

Sausage
Pasteurize by Thickness

Shank
Chop-Like: For 1 to 2 days
Braise-Like:
   156°F (68.8°C) for 18 to 24 hours
   165°F (73.9°C) for 18 to 24 hours
   176°F (80.0°C) for 12 to 18 hours

Shoulder
Chop-Like: For 1 to 2 days
Braise-Like:
   156°F (68.8°C) for 18 to 24 hours
   165°F (73.9°C) for 18 to 24 hours
   176°F (80.0°C) for 12 to 18 hours

Sirloin Chops
Chop-Like: For 6 to 12 hours

Sirloin Roast
Chop-Like: For 6 to 12 hours

Spare Ribs
Chop-Like: For 1 to 2 days
Braise-Like:
   156°F (68.8°C) for 18 to 24 hours
   165°F (73.9°C) for 18 to 24 hours
   176°F (80.0°C) for 12 to 18 hours

Spleen
Chop-Like: Pasteurize by Thickness

Tenderloin
Chop-Like: Pasteurize by Thickness

Chicken and Poultry Times and Temperatures

For more information about sous viding chicken and poultry, please refer to the Chicken, Duck and Poultry chapter.

Chicken, Turkey and Other "Well Done" Poultry

Breast
All should be pasteurized by thickness
Medium-Rare: 137°F (58°C)
Ideal: 141°F (60.5°C)
Medium-Well: 149°F (65°C)

Leg / Drumstick
Medium: 141°F (60.5°C) for 4 to 6 hours
Ideal: 148°F (64.4°C) for 4 to 6 hours
Shreddable: 165°F (73.9°C) for 8 to 12 hours

Sausage
All should be pasteurized by thickness
White Meat: 141°F (60.5°C)
Dark Meat: 148°F (64.4°C)
Mixed Meat: 141°F (60.5°C)

Thigh
Medium: 141°F (60.5°C) for 4 to 6 hours
Ideal: 148°F (64.4°C) for 4 to 6 hours
Shreddable: 165°F (73.9°C) for 8 to 12 hours

Whole Bird
Not recommended, but if you do try to spatchcock it to remove the air pocket or it could harbor bacteria during the cooking process. For all temperatures it should be pasteurized by thickness.
Medium: 141°F (60.5°C)
Medium-Well: 149°F (65°C)

Duck, Goose and "Medium Rare" Poultry

Breast
Rare: 125°F (51.6°C) by thickness
Medium-Rare: 131°F (55°C) by thickness
Medium: 140°F (60°C) by thickness

Leg
Medium-Rare: 131°F (55°C) for 3 to 6 hours
Medium: 140°F (60°C) for 3 to 6 hours
Confit: 167°F (75°C) for 10 to 20 hours

Sausage
131°F (55°C) by thickness

Thigh
Medium-Rare: 131°F (55°C) for 3 to 6 hours
Medium: 140°F (60°C) for 3 to 6 hours
Confit: 167°F (75°C) for 10 to 20 hours

Whole Bird
Not recommended, but if you do try to spatchcock it to remove the air pocket. For all temperatures it should be heated by thickness.
Medium-Rare: 131°F (55°C) for 3 to 6 hours
Medium: 140°F (60°C) for 3 to 6 hours

Eggs

The timing will change based on the size of the egg. The times below are for an average-sized American Large Grade A egg.

"Raw" Pasteurized Eggs
131°F (55°C) for 75 to 90 minutes

Soft Boiled / Poached
140°F to 145°F (60°C to 62.8°C) for 40 to 60 minutes
167°F (75°C) for 13 minutes

Semi-Hard
150°F (65.6°C) for 40 to 60 minutes

Hard Boiled
165°F (73.9°C) for 40 to 60 minutes

Fish and Shellfish Times and Temperatures

For more information about sous viding fish and shellfish, please refer to the Fish and Shellfish chapter.

Fish

Most fish follow the below temperatures pretty well, but different fish may be preferable at different temperatures.

> Warning: All of the fish you use should be high quality fish you would feel comfortable eating raw. The times and temperatures used are almost never enough to pasteurize them.

General Fish Times

All cook times should be based on the thickness, which is about:

0.5" (13mm) thick for 14 minutes
1" (25mm) thick for 35 minutes
1.5" (38mm) thick for 1 hour 25 minutes
2" (50mm) thick for 2 hours

General Fish Temperatures
Slightly Warmed: 104°F (40°C)
Firm Sashimi: 110°F (43.3°C)
Lightly Flaky and/or Firm: 120°F (48.9°C)
Very Flaky and/or Firm: 132°F (55.5°C)
Chewy: 140°F (60°C)

Shellfish

Shellfish varies greatly depending on the type you are trying to cook. Here are times and temperatures for some of the more common ones.

Crab
132°F (55.5°C) for 30 to 60 minutes
140°F (60°C) for 30 to 60 minutes

Lobster
The Serious Eats guide to lobster[28] is a great resource.
Low Temp: 115°F (46.1°C) for 20 to 40 minutes
Medium: 122°F (50°C) for 20 to 40 minutes
Ideal: 130°F (54°C) for 20 to 40 minutes
Very Firm: 140°F (60°C) for 20 to 40 minutes
Ideal Claw: 150°F (65.5°C) for 20 to 40 minutes

Octopus
Slow Cook: 170°F (76.6°C) for 4 to 8 hours
Fast Cook: 180°F (82.2°C) for 2 to 4 hours

Scallops
122°F (50°C) for 15 to 35 minutes
131°F (55°C) for 15 to 35 minutes

Shrimp
Sushi-Like: 122°F (50°C) for 15 to 35 minutes
Tender: 131°F (55°C) for 15 to 35 minutes
Firm: 140°F (60°C) for 15 to 35 minutes

Squid
Pre-Sear: 113°F (45°C) for 45 to 60 minutes
Low Heat: 138°F (58.9°C) for 2 to 4 hours
High Heat: 180°F (82.2°C) for 1 to 2 hours

Fruit and Vegetable Times and Temperatures

Almost all vegetables are cooked at 183°F (83.9°C) or higher and all entries below assume that temperature, unless otherwise stated. Hotter temperatures will cook the vegetables more quickly, but they will basically have the same texture at the end. There is also a lot of variability in a specific type of vegetable, with both their ripeness, variety, and size having an impact. So times can vary across vegetables, even of the same type.

Acorn Squash 1 to 2 hours
Apples 1 to 2 hours
Artichokes 45 to 75 minutes
Asparagus 10 to 30 minutes
Banana 10 to 15 minutes
Beet 60 to 90 minutes
Broccoli 30 to 60 minutes
Brussels Sprouts 45 to 60 minutes
Butternut Squash 45 to 60 minutes
Cabbage 60 minutes
Carrot 45 to 60 minutes
Cauliflower
    Florets 20 to 30 minutes
    For Puree 2 hours
    Stems 60 to 75 minutes
Celery Root 60 to 75 minutes
Chard 60 to 75 minutes
Cherries 15 to 25 minutes
Corn 15 to 25 minutes
Eggplant 30 to 45 minutes
Fennel 30 to 60 minutes
Golden Beets 30 to 60 minutes
Green Beans 30 to 45 minutes
Leek 30 to 60 minutes
Onion 35 to 60 minutes

Parsnip 30 to 60 minutes
Pea Pods 30 to 40 minutes
Peaches 30 to 60 minutes
Pears 25 to 60 minutes
Pineapple 167°F (75.0°C) for 45 to 60 minutes
Plums 167°F (75.0°C) for 15 to 20 minutes
Potatoes
    Small 30 to 60 minutes
    Large 60 to 120 minutes
Pumpkin 45 to 60 minutes
Radish 10 to 25 minutes
Rhubarb 141°F (60.6°C) for 25 to 45 minutes
Rutabaga 2 hours
Salsify 45 to 60 minutes
Squash
    Summer 30 to 60 minutes
    Winter 1 to 2 hours
Sunchokes 40 to 60 minutes
Sweet Potatoes
    Small 45 to 60 minutes
    Large 60 to 90 minutes
Swiss Chard 60 to 75 minutes
Turnip 45 to 60 minutes
Yams 30 to 60 minutes
Zucchini 30 to 60 minutes

Recipe Index

Red Meat
Beef
Hanger Steak with Succotash 75
Chuck Steak with Asparagus and Shishito Peppers 76
Short Rib Korean Lettuce Wraps 78
Smoked Brisket with Bourbon BBQ Sauce 80

Lamb
Rack of Lamb with Pomegranate and Brussels Sprouts 82

Bison
Bison Strip Steak Carbonara 84

Pork and Boar
Pork Chop w/ Broccolini and Roasted Peppers 91
Italian Sausage with Onions and Peppers 92
Sous Vide St. Louis Ribs 93
Pulled Pork with Chile Pepper BBQ Sauce 94
Boar Tenderloin with Cherry Chutney 96

Chicken, Duck and Poultry
Chicken
Spring Salad with Chicken Breast 104
Honey-Sriracha Glazed Chicken Legs 106

Turkey
Turkey Breast w/ Roasted Apples and Tomatoes 108

Duck
Duck Breast with Blackberry Port 110
Shredded Duck Legs with Sesame Noodles 112

Fish and Shellfish
Shrimp and Quinoa Bowl 119
Swordfish in Dashi with Snow Peas 120
Sea Bass with Microgreens and Mustard Oil 122
Sesame Crusted Tuna with Avocado Salad 124
Lobster Tail with Tomato and Corn Salad 126

Vegetables and Fruits
Asparagus with Dijon Mustard Vinaigrette 131
Miso Glazed Turnips 132
Curried Butternut Squash Soup 134
Chipotle Sweet Potato Salad 136
Apple Bourbon-Maple Chutney 137
Blueberry Compote 138

Infusions
Strawberry Basil Infused Rum 143
Citrus Infused Oil 144
Cherry Vanilla Infused Balsamic Vinegar 145

Eggs
13 Minute Egg on Wilted Spinach 149
Egg Cup Bites 150

Dairy, Sugar, and Custards
Cinnamon-Vanilla Crème Brulee 154
Yogurt 156

Did You Enjoy This Book?

Most Popular Modernist Recipes

Here are some of my most popular modernist recipes.

AmazingFoodMadeEasy.com

If you are looking for sous vide recipes, detailed equipment reviews, in-depth articles, or just some inspiration, my website has you covered.

In addition to sous vide, I also cover other aspects of modernist cooking, including the whipping siphon, making foams and gels, and even infusions and spherification. Come check out how you can expand your cooking tool kit!

Modernist Cooking Made Easy: Sous Vide

Modernist Cooking Made Easy: Sous Vide is the best selling sous vide book available and the authoritative guide to low temperature precision cooking and it will help make sous vide a part of your everyday cooking arsenal.

The bulk of this book is the more than 85 recipes it contains. Designed so you can skim the recipes, looking for something that inspires you, or turn to a specific recipe to learn all about how to cook the cut of meat it features.

Modernist Cooking Made Easy: The Whipping Siphon

The whipping siphon is probably my second favortie tool after my sous vide machine. There are so many great things you can do with it and my book focuses on the three main uses: Foaming, Infusing, and Carbonating. It delivers the information you need to understand how the techniques work and provides you with over 50 recipes to illustrate these techniques while allowing you to create great dishes that will delight everyone that tries them!

Modernist Cooking Made Easy: Infusions

The ultimate guide to crafting flavorful infusions using both modernist and traditional techniques. Exploring this process allows you to create many wonderful dishes, from custom cocktails and personalized sodas to flavorful vinaigrettes and sauces.

Discover how to create vibrant and amazing infusions that will amaze your family and friends!

About the Author

Jason Logsdon is a passionate home cook who loves to try new things, exploring everything from sous vide and whipping siphons to blow torches, foams, spheres and infusions. He has self published 9 cookbooks which have sold over 60,000 copies in paperback and electronic formats. His books include a best seller that hit the #1 spot on Amazon for Slow Cooking and #2 spot on Gourmet Cooking. He also runs AmazingFoodMadeEasy.com, one of the largest modernist cooking websites, and SelfPublishACookbook.com, a website dedicated to helping food bloggers successfully navigate the self publishing process.

Endnotes

1) https://www.facebook.com/groups/1735055260073124/
2) http://AFMEasy.com/SVEquip
3) http://www.amazingfoodmadeeasy.com/info/modernist-cooking-blog/more/how-to-use-ziploc-bags-for-sous-vide
4) http://AFMEasy.com/SVCircs
5) http://AFMEasy.com/SVBenchmarks
6) http://modernistcuisine.com/2013/03/is-it-safe-cook-plastic/
7) http://blog.chefsteps.com/2014/09/5-common-misconceptions-about-sous-vide-cooking/
8) http://AFMEasy.com/Ruler
9) http://www.douglasbaldwin.com/sous-vide.html
10) http://www.amazingfoodmadeeasy.com/info/modernist-cooking-blog/more/how-does-temperature-affect-meat
11) http://AFMEasy.com/Recipes
12) http://AFMEasy.com/Marinate
13) http://www.amazingfoodmadeeasy.com/info/modernist-cooking-blog/more/polyscience-300-series-chamber-vacuum-sealer-detailed-review
14) https://www.chefsteps.com/activities/a-complete-guide-to-sous-vide-packaging-safety-sustainability-and-sourcing
15) http://bit.ly/2jI44a3
16) http://www.recyclingnj.com/recycle/plastic.html
17) http://io9.gizmodo.com/how-to-recognize-the-plastics-that-are-hazardous-to-you-461587850
18) http://www.csrecycling.co.uk/news-how-to-identify-different-types-of-plastic-39
19) http://AFMEasy.com/Torches
20) http://AFMEasy.com/IceBathTest
21) http://www.deadrabbitnyc.com/
22) http://www.blueprintbrooklyn.com/
23) http://www.amazingfoodmadeeasy.com/tags/cocktail-books
24) https://www.chefsteps.com/activities/the-egg-calculator
25) http://www.seriouseats.com/2013/10/sous-vide-101-all-about-eggs.html
26) http://www.douglasbaldwin.com/sous-vide.html#The_Mathematics_of_Sous_Vide
27) http://forums.egullet.org/index.php?//topic/136274-sous-vide-index/
28) http://www.seriouseats.com/2016/12/food-lab-complete-guide-to-sous-vide-lobster.html

www.ingramcontent.com/pod-product-compliance
Lightning Source LLC
LaVergne TN
LVHW061345060426
835512LV00012B/2564